World's Best
Jewish Humor

WORLD'S BEST
JEWISH HUMOR

A. Stanley Kramer

Illustrations by Richard Zorn

A Citadel Press Book

Published by Carol Publishing Group

A Citadel Press Book
Published by Carol Publishing Group
Citadel Press is a registered trademark of Carol Communications, Inc.
Editorial Offices: 600 Madison Avenue, New York, N.Y. 10022
Sales and Distribution Offices: 120 Enterprise Avenue, Secaucus, N.J. 07094
In Canada: Canadian Manda Group, P.O. Box 920, Station U, Toronto, Ontario M8Z 5P9
Queries regarding rights and permissions should be addressed to Carol Publishing Group, 600 Madison Avenue, New York, N.Y. 10022

Carol Publishing Group books are available at special discounts for bulk purchases, sales promotion, fund-raising, or educational purposes. Special editions can be created to specifications. For details, contact: Special Sales Department, Carol Publishing Group, 120 Enterprise Avenue, Secaucus, N.J. 07094

Book design by Ardashes Hamparian

Manufactured in the United States of America

10   9   8   7   6   5   4   3   2   1

Library of Congress Cataloging-in-Publication Data

Kramer, A. Stanley
  World's best Jewish humor / A. Stanley Kramer
      p.   cm.
  "A Citadel Press book."
  ISBN 0-8065-1503-1
  1. Jewish wit and humor. 2. Proverbs, Jewish. I. Title.
PN6231.J5K72   1994
398.9′089924—dc20   93-45498
                                    CIP

Contents

An Appreciation

Producing a book—an anthology or any other of real substance—is far from a solitary job. In addition to the author, grinding away at his desk or machine, there are all those others, living and dead, who are essential to the project—particularly the writers before him who have provided much of the substance of the new work.

First, there is that great scholar, researcher, and raconteur, Leo Rosten, whom I must thank for his three unparalleled tomes on Jewish humor: *The Joys of Yiddish, Hooray for Yiddish*, and *The Joys of Yinglish*. The research, scholarship, editing, and all-around brilliance that characterizes these books is mind-boggling. Also they saved me a thousand years of original research (I should live so long!).

Then there is the profundity, erudition, and thoroughness of editor, writer, and translator Nathan Ausubel, whose *A Treasury of Jewish Humor* and *A Treasury of Jewish Folklore* opened for me new and revealing vistas of life in Europe's shtetls.

Next (and these are in no particular order) there is the incredibly comprehensive *Big Book of Jewish Humor*, edited and annotated by William Novak and Moshe Waldocks—a modern milestone of completeness, including absolutely convulsing cartoons along with a text that could crack a smile on the Sphinx.

There are the many, many laugh books of the late Bennett Cerf; Fred Kogo's *Yiddish Slang and Idioms*; Earl Wilson's *The Bathroom Reader*, Louis Untermeyer's *A Treasury of Laughter;* Robert Orben's *Joke Teller's Handbook; The Best of Henny Youngman; Life Is With People* by Mark Zborowski and Ruth Herzog; *Jewish Wry* by Sarah B. Cohen; and *The Best of Sholom Aleichem*.

Impossible to acknowledge individually are the thousand-and-one (an inadequate cliché, actually there are many more) radio and TV programs; tapes, records, cartoons, newspaper, and magazine articles; columnists, vaudeville, and borscht-belt skits; movies, novels, and short stories; jokes told at parties and gatherings, etcetera, over more than sixty years—and which have been absorbed into my very bloodstream.

For all this (plus a retentive memory) I am deeply grateful. For no one starts from the ground up in selecting, editing, and presenting a long tradition of humor—although each selects and presents it in his or her own way. Always we begin from the elevated platform erected by our predecessors.

I owe much to my friends, who contributed by supporting me with stories and suggestions (frequently useless as material but emotionally sustaining). Among these friends are members of my family, none of whom have ever written more than a personal letter, who asked each other in puzzlement if people would actually pay money for such stuff.

Heading the parade is my wife, Edith, whose sensitivity and common sense have prevented me from making the kind of bullheaded gaffes to which I am prone. In addition, she is undoubtedly the world's best speller, far outstripping my fancy electronic typewriter whose Wordspell merely squeaks when I misspell a word but never gives me the correct spelling—as Edith always does. Her taking all phone calls, shooing away unwanted callers; keeping me socially uninvolved; feeding, comforting, and cosseting me; the while somehow managing the shopping and housekeeping—all this burnishes the halo she has long worn.

Only my religion prevents me from nominating her for sainthood.

For invaluable assistance in securing materials from everywhere and trying them out on their friends and each other, I thank my three closest friends, lifetime jokesters, and fellow collectors of Jewish humor. They are: Ernest Cheslow, Edwin Weinshelbaum, and Leonard Elliot.

At my age I should be thankful, too, for an unsoured sense of humor and the physical energy for completing this work.

Thanks, Lord.

A. Stanley Kramer

Preface

Any preamble to a volume of Jewish humor might well first define the nature of the Jews themselves. There have been many such definitions, but perhaps no one has described them more vividly than a non-Jew, Mark Twain, in *Harper's Monthly* of September 1899:

> If the statistics are right, the Jews constitute but one quarter of one percent of the human race. It suggests a nebulous dim puff of stardust lost in the blaze of the Milky Way. Properly, the Jew ought hardly to be heard of, but he is heard of, has always been heard of. He is as prominent on the planet as any other people, and his importance is extravagantly out of proportion to the smallness of his bulk.
>
> His contribution to the world's list of great names in literature, science, art, music, finance, medicine and abstruse learning are very out of proportion to the weakness of his numbers. He has made a marvelous fight in this world in all ages; and he has done it with his hands tied behind him. He could be vain of himself and be excused for it. The Egyptians, the Babylonians and the Persians rose, filled the planet with sound and splendor, then faded to dream-stuff and passed away; the Greeks and the Romans followed and made a vast noise, and they were gone; other peoples have sprung up and held their torch high for a time but it burned out, and they sit in the twilight now, or have vanished.
>
> The Jew saw them all, survived them all, and is now what he always was, exhibiting no decadence, no infir-

mities of age, no weakening of his parts, no slowing of his energies, no dulling of his alert and aggressive mind. All things are mortal but the Jews; all other forces pass, but he remains.

A Great Mystery presents itself: Why has so much and such *great* humor come from this oppressed, driven, dispersed minority of largely Ashkenazic, or Eastern European, Jews? Are poverty, oppression, and insecurity the deepest wellsprings of humor? Why does the persecuted Jew continue to laugh and make the rest of the world laugh with him?

Sigmund Freud, generally considered a very serious man, found his release in telling jokes to a wide audience. His analysis of Jewish humor concluded that "self-mockery" was its most distinguishing feature.

Actually, Jewish humor is much more than that. There is nothing alien in it for the rest of mankind. It is universal while still maintaining its own bittersweet flavor. In the many lands where Jews lived, they survived incredible persecution and poverty, so that in their humor, comedy and tragedy are inextricable. *Yaschekas*, or "laughter through tears," Jewish folk writers call it—the *"oy vay!"* and the "ha-ha!" combined.

Whether they are about nineteenth-century shtetl Jews or modern American Jews, Jewish jokes largely concern adversity—about which Jews are certainly mavens. This is a kind of self-protection; by laughing at the absurdities, the cruelties, and injustices of life, much of the pain is deadened.

Jewish humor is usually not cruel, although it is often ironic. Jewish laughter is *with* people rather than at them. The Jewish joker is more than a hardened cynic. He is a philosopher, filled with indulgent laughter at the silly, and often mean, antics of the entire human race. To him the poor individual is caught up in *meshuggeneh velt*, a crazy world to which we are all confined.

Whether ancient or modern, Jewish humor largely concerns itself with a relatively few but universal topics: family, food, business, poverty, wealth, sickness, religion, and survival. It is often self-critical, even self-deprecating; frequently anti-establishment, ridiculing pomposity and pretense. It delights in exposing phoneys and strongly stresses the dignity and worth of "little" people. It is definitely the humor of the common man.

Yet, paradoxically, for such deeply religious people, the Jews are highly irreverent in their humor and do not hesitate to talk to God one-to-one, criticizing, arguing with the Almighty's handling of human affairs and recommending sometimes drastic improvements.

Jewish humor falls naturally into two major categories: 1) traditional—that of the nineteenth-century European shtetl; and 2) twentieth-century American.

The traditional is mostly folk humor—broad jokes, funny stories, and epigrams—mostly anonymous, some of it floating around seemingly forever; told and retold ad infinitum so that its authorship is lost in the mists of time. (Some of it is far older than the nineteenth century and can be traced to 1300 or before!)

Twentieth-century (American) Jewish humor is of far wider scope, and it's much harder to define the degree of "Jewishness," largely diluted because of the differences in the backgrounds and mores of the immigrants themselves, as generation after generation becomes more assimilated. New subjects for jokes sprang up as the old ones faded. *Shnorrers* lost relevance. American Jews laughed about name-changing, Reform Judaism, intermarriages, fund-raising, Seventh Avenue, Jewish-American mothers, new style (ignorant) rabbis, and the nouveaux riches.

Our burgeoning technology provided a veritable humor explosion, providing wider outlets than were ever provided by the early phonograph records (*Cohen on the Telephone*), vaudeville, the Yiddish theater, newspapers, and a few magazines. There was the borscht belt, Broadway, nightclubs, cartoons, the movies, radio, more and better recordings, TV, cassettes, compact discs, and tape.

This is a new *all-star collection* of Jewish humor, painstakingly selected from among all that has gone before—in our admittedly biased opinion, the best of the lot—modernized and rewritten for maximum impact.

It *is not* a collection of *new* jokes. There aren't enough *new* Jewish jokes of any caliber to make even a pamphlet. These are rather *"the Champs."*

But neither is it any clip-and-paste job. Jokes have to be freshened to fit the times—rephrased and dressed with this season's lapels and hemlines. Here are all the rib-tickling situations, ambiguities, philosophic reflections, plays-upon-words—basic, universal, and timeless. The costumes and backgrounds are often new, but the plots and players are satisfyingly familiar.

This collection benefits from the scholars and writers who have preceded us, each adding to the mother lode his own brilliance and imagination—borrowing and adapting from one another and from one medium to another—some going as far back as the twelfth century: the Zohar and the Talmud itself.

* * *

Jewish jokes, like all others, are part of an oral tradition, face-to-face, far better told than written. Nothing is as good as facing a live audience, where the impact of a joke can be mightily reinforced by the right tone of voice, pauses and inflections, expressions, gestures, body language. This is just as true of the jokes here. There will be some that tickle you more than others, you'll get a second charge out of telling them. Don't hesitate. We never did. Put in your personal touches and whatever little details seem appropriate. If you're any good at some particular dialect, use it. Practice it first if you have to. We haven't attempted to reproduce dialects or accents here. That's your province. We hope there's enough ham in you to try.

But whether you do or not, we hope you enjoy this collection of Jewish humor as much as we did putting it together.

Enjoy! Enjoy!

World's Best
Jewish Humor

1

Yiddish— The *Mama-Loshen*

Yiddish is the vernacular spoken by Jews all over the world. Before the Holocaust, 11 million (about two-thirds of all the Jews in the world) were supposed to have understood Yiddish. Today it is widely feared to be a disappearing language, despite the strenuous efforts of scholars to revive it.

Most European and early U.S. immigrant jokes, fables, and funny stories were written in Yiddish, but not all. A small percent were written in Hebrew, German, Spanish, Dutch, Arabic, Russian, French, and Hungarian.

By now most of the better jokes and stories have been translated into English, including many in this book. But, by sheer weight of numbers, Yiddish is the true Mama-Loshen or Mother Tongue, the daily language of European Jewish communities.

Yiddish is frequently confused with Hebrew, the Jew's language of prayer, sacred writings, and religious ceremonies as well as the official language of Israel. The confusion arises because Yiddish uses the letters of the Hebrew alphabet, and also reads from right to left. Moreover, its spelling (standardized) is phonetic.

Probably only twenty percent of the Yiddish vocabulary is made up of Hebrew words and phrases. For Yiddish and Hebrew are as separate as Hungarian and English. Much of the Yiddish vocabulary is adapted from Russian, Romanian, Ukrainian, several Slovene dialects, and, in the last hundred or more years, English.

Even with its diminishing usage, Yiddish keeps growing by accretion. It is older than modern German and much older than modern English. It comes down to us from Germany and the north of France of nearly a thousand years ago. There, Jews absorbed the local vernacular, writing German in their Hebrew alphabet, phonetically—just as they used Hebrew letters to write several other languages. (Latin, and its alphabet, was, however, rigorously avoided because of its association with all things Christian and anti-Jewish.)

Yiddish is basically a Germanic tongue embellished with Hebrew words and phrases (particularly names, holy days, and all religious or ritualistic matters). As the Jews migrated from country to country, Yiddish accumulated many words from other languages. It expanded in the ghettos and thrived, becoming the native tongue of the Ashkenazim, or Eastern European Jews.

A digression is indicated here, for there was (and is) another "Jewish" language, the language of the Sephardic Jews of Spain and Portugal. Sephardic Judaism dominated Jewish culture from about A.D. 600 until the Jews were expelled from Spain in 1492. This Judaism was a complex blend of Talmudic thinking, Greek philosophy, Aristotelianism, what little science then existed, and the ideas of a distinguished Islamic scholar—one Averroës.

Speaking their own vernacular, Ladino, rather than Yiddish, the Sephardim differ from the Ashkenazim in many customs as well as in the order and text of their prayers and in the intonation of the synagogue chants.

The use of Yiddish today is directly correlated with age; more older Jews understand it than young ones, despite continuing efforts by scholars to keep it alive. Today more Jews *understand* Yiddish than speak it; more can speak it than read it. And, definitely, more can manage to read it than write it.

With its multilingual roots, Yiddish is incredibly rich in descriptions and imagery and movingly expresses every shade and nuance of feeling. It has an incomparable vocabulary of praises, curses, and expletives—as well as a powerful arsenal of descriptive names that beggars many more sophisticated languages.

There exists a tremendous wealth of Yiddish literature: stories, plays, novels, essays, and poems. Much has been translated, but because of the lower explosive content of the English language, much has suffered in translation.

See Appendix A at the back of this book for a comprehensive list of nineteenth-century Jewish humor writers, most of whom wrote in Yiddish.

Curses and Imprecations

Jewish humor expresses its earthy character in a wide variety of vivid invocations for someone's personal disaster. Shtetl dwellers hurled epithets at each other and at their oppressors, rather than blaspheme. For, amongst Jews, taking the name of God was a serious transgression and they never God-damned anyone. Fist-fighting was also definitely non-Jewish. Instead, men (and women!) fought with their wits, with sharp tongues and vivid imaginations—giving vent to all the steam inevitably arising from poverty and persecution.

I like to think that these curses were seldom meant literally, they were so wild, fanciful, and violent. Sometimes they must have been given with a smile that belied their words, with no actual violence intended. And sometimes they were screamed with red-faced fury at an offender who could not be reached in any other way. (And, probably just as often, mumbled under the breath for fear of reprisal.)

In the pinched closeness of small-village life, these imprecations were especially suitable for telling off cruel, mean, stingy, or otherwise obnoxious neighbors.

Here are a few, in no particular order, ranging from the pedestrian: "Get killed!" to the highly imaginative: "May your blood turn to whiskey so that a hundred bedbugs get drunk on it and dance the mazurka in your belly button!"

With some of the following curses we have given their

phonetic Yiddish equivalents. Do try a few aloud. Their very sounds are vehement and malicious, as no English translation possibly can be.

- A plague on you!—*"A choleria ahf dir!"*
- You should choke on it!—*Der shtikt zols tu veren!"*
- He should grow like an onion with his head in the ground!—*Er sol vaksen vi tsibiliss mit dem kop in drerd!*
- Go split your guts!—*Gai plotz!*
- Onions should grow from your navel!—*Zoll vaksen tzibiliss fun pupik!*
- You should swell up like a mountain!—*Zolst geshvollen veren vi a barg!*
- May a trolleycar grow in your stomach!
- Go fornicate yourself!
- Shove it up your rectum!—*Zolst es shtupin in tochis arein!*
- You should get a stomach cramp!
- May you back into a pitchfork and grab a hot stove for support!
- May your bones be broken as often as the ten commandments!
- May all your teeth fall out except one—so you can have a toothache!
- May you be known for your hospitality to God's creatures: lice, rats, bedbugs, fleas, worms and maggots!
- You should burn like a wick and they should put you out with benzine!

A Dozen S's—All Bad!

In Yiddish there is a word—rarely two or three—that means a certain kind of person—what he is or what he does. For example there is a word for:

> - A hero
> - A fine fellow

- A genius
- A scholar
- A teacher
- A merchant
- A fighter
- A cantor
- A farmer
- A peasant
- A matchmaker, etcetera.

Each condition, nature, or occupation has a name. And that's it—insofar as *acceptable* natures, conditions, and occupations are concerned. But when it come to *undesirable* persons, the assortment of derogatory names for them is legion. The very sound of such names is harsh, uncomplimentary. Names like: *yold, paskudnyak,* or *nudnik.* Their precise definitions are extremely flexible and often overlap. Say any of them aloud and even a tone-deaf person can tell they are not complimentary.

  As a case in point, here are twelve undesirable kinds of people, together with an abbreviation of what a Yiddish-English dictionary says about them:

Shlemiel	a simpleton; fall guy; pip-squeak; naive one; untidy person; clumsy one; social misfit.
Shlepper	a drag; drip, jerk; beggar; petty thief; untidy one, down-at-the-heels person.
Shmegegge	an untalented, petty person; maladroit one; a drip; a whiner.
Shmendrick	a Milquetoast; pip-squeak; wet-behind-the-ears, weakling; thin, small.
Shlimazl	a born loser; a chronically unlucky person.
Shlock	a disagreeable, peevish person; a slob; a whiner.
Shlump	a drip; a drag; a wet blanket.
Shmo	fall guy; boob; clumsy one; unlucky; a jerk.
Shmuck	a penis (prick); dope; jerk; boob; son of a bitch.
Shnook	sad sack; pathetic fellow; timid one; meek; a patsy.

| *Shnorrer* | moocher; beggar; panhandler; chiseler; bum; drifter; bargainer. |
| *Shtunk* | a stinker; nasty person; fool; dope; jerk; ingrate. |

And these are only the S's!

Common Expressions Read and Heard Every Day—Inspired by If Not Directly Translated From Yiddish

Many Yiddish words, unchanged, have insinuated themselves into the English language—usually via the performances or writings of Jewish comedians. Words like: *shlep, nosh, gonif, shlemiel,* and so on. But Yiddish has had a much wider impact than the absorption of these words alone. These are the idioms, the literal translations of Yiddish expressions into colloquialisms—often ungrammatical but usually pungent expressions that spice our daily speech. Here are a few:

- Look who's talking.
- Go do her something.
- This I need yet?
- Go fight City Hall.
- Don't ask!
- What's the bottom line?
- On him it looks good.
- It shouldn't happen to a dog.
- Eat your heart out.
- *Big* deal!
- Excuse the expression.
- Could be.
- Go hit your head against the wall.
- You should live so long.
- Do him something.
- Okay by me.
- Get lost!
- I need it like a hole in the head.
- From *that* he makes a living?
- Who *needs* it?
- He knows from nothing.
- *All right* already.

2

One-Liners, Except When They Run a Little More

One-Liners

A potpourri of aphorisms, apothegms, axioms, bon-mots, epigrams, proverbs, witticisms—with a few very ancient poems thrown in.

These are some from every age and point of view—from the thirteenth century, the Zohar (a fantastic collection of cabalistic superstitions and folklore) to last night's TV comic. Some more accurately belong under "Wit" than humor, as there is nothing rib-tickling about them. You've probably heard a few, or variations thereof. And, if you're like most of us, credited the wrong authors as often as not. For instance, you'll be surprised to see that many that sound like Shakespeare (he is *not* represented) are really from the Talmud.

Even when these short-shots don't make you laugh, many will make you think—for which there is no extra charge.

■   ■   ■

It's not that money makes everything good—it's that no money makes everything bad.—Folk saying

■

Give every man the benefit of the doubt.—Talmud

11

The ignorant cannot be pious.—Ibid.

■

Look at the contents, not the bottle.—Ibid.

■

Don't threaten the child; either punish or forgive him.—Ibid.

■

If you must strike a child, use a string.—Ibid.

■

If all men were students of philosophy, the social order would be destroyed and the human race quickly exterminated.
—Maimonides

■

Whenever there is too much, something is lacking.—Anon.

■

The real "Jewish Question" is this: From what can a Jew earn a living?—Sholem Aleichem

■

When two divorced people get married, four get into bed.
—Folk saying

■

Every Jew has his own brand of madness.—Folk saying

■

Only the doctor suffers from good health.—Folk saying

■

A widower is the only man whose wife is an angel.—Folk saying

■

A sordid money-grubber is anyone making more money than you.—Anon.

Old age is when your comb has more hair than you—and more teeth.—Anon.

■

Gratitude is the anticipation of future favors.—Anon.

■

A friend is one who loves you in spite of your virtues.—Folk saying

■

A *goy* is anyone who pays retail prices.—Anon.

■

A self-made man is one who admires his maker.—Anon.

■

A second marriage is the triumph of hope over experience.—Anon.

■

Tears are the world's greatest water power.—Folk saying

■

One fool can ask more questions than ten wise men can answer.—Anon.

■

The man who marries for money earns it.—Talmud

■

One good deed leads to another.—Ibid.

■

Begin a lesson with a humorous illustration.—Ibid.

■

Bad neighbors count a man's income but not his expenses.—Ibid.

Judge a man not by the words of his mother but from the comments of his neighbors.—Ibid.

■

When in a city follow its customs.—Ibid.

■

All is well that ends well.—Ibid.

■

A rabbi whose congregation does not want to drive him out of town isn't a rabbi; and a rabbi they do drive out isn't a man. —Based on a saying in the Talmud

■

When a scholar goes out in search of a bride, he should take an ignoramus along with him as an expert.—Talmud

■

"For instance" is not proof.—Folk saying

■

Bygone tsouris are good to relate.—Folk saying

■

Troubles are partial to wetness—to tears and whiskey.—Folk saying

■

When you baptize a Jew, hold him under water for five minutes.—Bulgarian proverb

■

Man comes into the world with an *"Oy!"* and leaves with a *"Gevalt!"*—Proverb

■

He who has been bitten by a snake will be scared of a piece of rope.—Anon.

Yom Kippur—sometimes called "Instant Lent."—Anon.

∎

It is the way of a dog that, if he is hit by a stone, he bites a fellow dog.—The Zohar

∎

The most important thing a writer's got to have? A small appetite.—Anon.

∎

If you're lucky, everyone says you're smart.—Anon.

∎

Love is sweet, but it's tastier with bread.—Anon.

∎

When does a poor man eat chicken? When he is sick, or else when the chicken is.—Anon.

∎

The best part about telling the truth is that you don't have to remember what you said.—Anon.

∎

A stingy person and a fat cow are useful only after they are dead.—Sholem Aleichem

∎

Music played at weddings always reminds me of the music played for soldiers before they go off to battle.—Heinrich Heine

∎

Some scholars are like bank tellers who carry the keys to the strong box that contains great sums of money that don't belong to them.—Ludwig Börne

∎

There are some people who may be compared to the small fashionable shops: All the merchandise is displayed in the show window.—Berthold Auerbach

■

There is much good in platonic love; it does not prevent a man from dreaming by day and sleeping by night. And anyway, it's so inexpensive.—Berthold Auerbach

■

I never think of the future; it comes soon enough.—Albert Einstein

■

Every woman should marry—and no man.—Benjamin Disraeli

■

The Jews are just like everyone else, only more so.—Anon.

■

An old maid who gets married becomes a young wife.—Anon.

■

One man chops all the wood, the other does all the grunting.— Folk saying

■

Your health comes first; you can always hang yourself later.— Folk saying

■

A man is not honest simply because he never had a chance to steal.—Folk saying

■

Poverty is no disgrace—which is the only good thing you can say about it.—Folk saying

■

Learning is the best merchandise.—Proverb

■

Don't ask the patient, ask the doctor.—Proverb

■

Many complain of their looks, but none complain of their brains.—Proverb

■

A *shadchen* is "a dealer in livestock."—Sholem Aleichem

■

A psychiatrist is a Jewish doctor who can't stand the sight of blood.—Anon.

■

Life is a dream for the wise, a game for the fool, a comedy for the rich, a tragedy for the poor.—Sholem Aleichem

■

Everyone sits in the prison of his own ideas.—Albert Einstein

■

God loves the poor but helps the rich.—Anon.

■

How to make a small fortune in Israel: Come with a large one.—Anon.

■

One father can support ten children, but ten children can't support one father.—Anon.

■

When a father helps a son, both smile; when a son helps a father, both cry.—Folk saying

■

Jewish dropout: A boy who didn't get his Ph.D.—Anon.

■

The longest road leads to the pocket.—Anon.

■

Ingenious ideas usually come like the fireman—too late.—Anon.

■

To a wedding you walk; to a divorce you run.—Anon.

■

All brides are beautiful; all corpses are pious.—Anon.

■

If you want to get a reputation as a wise man, agree with everybody.—Anon.

■

Little children won't let you sleep; big children won't let you live.—Anon.

■

When a man has *mazel* even his rooster lays eggs.—Anon.

■

As long as words are in your mouth, you are the master; the moment you utter them, you are their slave.—Ibn Gabirol

■

What is the sign of a fool? He talks too much.—The Zohar

■

If I am not for myself, who will be? And if I am only for myself, what am I? And if not now—when?—Hillel

■

Mothers understand what children do not say.—Anon.

A mother has glass eyes (she cannot see her children's faults).
—Anon.

■

No one ever goes to that restaurant—it's too crowded.—Anon.

■

If your father were alive, he'd turn over in his grave.—Anon.

■

Bachelor: A man who comes to work each morning from different directions.—Folk saying

■

If praying did any good, they would hire men to do it.—Folk saying

■

When you go to a restaurant, choose a table near a waiter.
—Anon.

■

The rich have heirs, not children.—Anon.

■

When you add to the truth, you subtract from it.—Anon.

■

What the Lord does is certainly best—probably.—Anon.

■

God is closest to those whose hearts are broken.—Anon.

■

Dear God: You help total *strangers*—so why not me?—Anon.

■

If you don't want to suffer in your old age, hang yourself while you're young.—Folk saying

If you rub elbows with the rich, you'll get a hole in your sleeve.
—Folk saying

■

When a Jew is right, he gets a beating.—Proverb

There is no Jew without his bundle of troubles.—Proverb

■

Thrift is the most desired virtue—in an ancestor.—Folk saying

Discussion is a method of confirming others in their errors.
—Anon.

■

Middle age is that time in life when a man would rather not have a good time than have to get over it.—Anon.

■

Marriage is a condition before which eyes should be kept open—and half shut afterward.—Folk saying

■

The cleverest woman finds a need for foolish admirers.—Anon.

■

Love makes of the wisest man a fool, and of the most foolish woman—a sage.—Moritz Saphir

■

Epitaph to a waiter: God caught his eye.—Anon.

■

People do not kill time—time kills them.—Moritz Saphir

■

It is easier to fight for one's principles than to live up to them.
—Alfred Adler

■

Love is a sweet dream and marriage is the alarm clock.—Anon.

■

When you've got a lot of money you're both wise and handsome—and my! how well you sing.—Anon.

■

Were the rich but able to hire others to die for them, poor people would be making a real nice living.—Anon.

The heart grows harder more quickly in riches than an egg in boiling water.—Ludwig Börne

■

He who in life has never made a fool of himself has also never been wise.—Heinrich Heine

■ ■ ■

THE DEPARTED PHYSICIAN

Isaac Benjacob (nineteenth century)

Our doctor is dead; ah well, dry your tears;
Death's sad, but what use to resent it?
For if he had lived for another few years,
There'd be none of us here to lament it.

■

A JEWISH BEGGAR'S COMPLAINT

*Anonymous Hebrew Poem
from France in the Middle Ages*

Greens on Sunday,
Crumbs and water Monday,
Onions Tuesday,
Left-over onions Wednesday,
Stale lentils Thursday,
Left-over lentils Friday;
While on the Sabbath it seems best
From meat and wine to take a rest.

SHLIMAZL

Abraham Ibn Ezra (twelfth century)

My labour is vain,
No wealth I gain.
My fate since birth,
Is gloom on earth.
If I sold shrouds,
No one would die.
If I sold lamps,
Then in the sky,
The sun, for spite,
Would shine at night.

THE MOUTH AND THE EARS
Shemtob Palquera (thirteenth century)

My friend, speak always once, but listen twice,
This, I would have you know, is sound advice:
For God has given you and all your peers
A single mouth, friend, but a pair of ears.

■

UNTITLED
Isaac Benjacob

Think not that those are purely sages
Whose beard and paunch are large of size.
Or else the goats through all the ages
Must, too, be classed among the wise.

■

King David and King Solomon
Lived merry, merry lives
With many, many lady friends
And many, many wives.

But when old age crept onward
With all its many qualms,
King Solomon wrote the Proverbs
And King David wrote the Psalms.

■

THE FIRST GRAY HAIR
Judah ha-Levi (twelfth century)

One day I saw a gray hair in my head.
I plucked it out when this to me it said:
Think, if thou wilt, that thou art rid of me,
I've twenty friends who soon will mock at thee.

An Epitaph

Isaac Benjacob

Here lies Nachshon, a man of great renown,
Who won much glory in his native town.
'Twas hunger that killed him, and they let him die.
They give him status now, and gaze and sigh—
While Nachshon lived, he badly wanted bread,
Now he's gone, he gets a stone instead.

■

Free

Sholem Aleichem (nineteenth century)

If one has no means of livelihood, he is free to die of hunger.
If one is unemployed, he is free to knock his head against
   the wall.
If one breaks a leg, he is free to walk on crutches.
If one gets married and hasn't enough to support his wife,
He is free to go begging alms with her from house to house.
If one dies, he is free to get buried.

■

Flea Song

Yehudah Al-Charizi (thirteenth century)

You ruthless flea, who desecrates my couch,
   And draw my blood to sate your appetite,
You know not rest, on Sabbath day or feast—
   Your feast it is when you can pinch and bite.

My friends expound the law: to kill a flea
   Upon the Sabbath day a sin they call;
But I prefer the other law that says,
   Be sure a murderer's malice to forestall.

3

Prominent in Jewish Humor: The Rabbi

A rabbi is not a priest or a minister the way a Catholic priest or a Protestant clergyman is. He is in no way an intermediary between God and man. His position gives him no status in any hierarchy, for there is no Jewish hierarchy. The rabbi's authority rests solely on his character, his learning, his personal qualities.

His lot is often not a happy one, for he is constantly criticized for what he does or doesn't do. Nahman of Bratzlav, an early nineteenth-century Chasidic writer, said, "It was hard for Satan to mislead the whole world, so he appointed prominent rabbis in different localities."

The rabbi is primarily a *teacher*. Moses is the prime example, the most important *teacher* of all. Religious Jews call Moses *Moishe Rabbenu*, which means "Our teacher, Moses."

Traditionally a rabbi teaches the Torah (the Old Testament), the Talmud, and later rabbinical works and attempts to apply their lessons to daily life. He is supposed to uplift the moral, ethical, and religious life of his congregation.

He performs the ceremonies for birth, confirmation, marriage, and death. He also oversees religious instruction, preaches sermons, offers comfort and consolation to the sick and bereaved, and guides the perplexed. He combines the functions of lecturer, counselor, and psychiatrist. Little wonder that he doesn't please everyone!

It is important to remember that the rabbi is not *imposed* upon his congregation but freely selected by them, with the attendant conflict between the two parties extant in most congregations:

(a) Our rabbi is the most wonderful man alive and shame on anyone who talks against him! and (b) We've got to get rid of this guy; he's not for us!

Lest you think rabbi-bashing is a modern invention, there is mention of it in the Talmud!

Originally rabbis were lay readers who made their living from something else. The great Hillel was a woodchopper, Ishmael was a tanner, Maimonides a physician, and Shammai a surveyor. It was only over the centuries that the rabbinate became a full-time (and paid) occupation.

Certainly the rabbi was never supposed to be a comedian or even prominent in humorous dialogue or situations. But as you will see, he very often was.

■　■　■

"Rabbi," asked the president of the congregation, "why is it that you, a man of God, are always talking about business matters, whereas I, a businessman, once I leave the office, talk only about spiritual matters?"

"This follows a very old and sound principle," answered the rabbi.

"What principle is that?"

"The principle that people usually like to discuss things they know nothing about."

■

An unsuccessful merchant in a poor Russian village came complaining to his rabbi. "Rabbi, I'm desperate. My roof is falling in and my wife and children are crying for bread. I can't seem to make a living. Tell me, what shall I do?" The rabbi stroked his beard and then answered.

"I advise you to become a seller of flour and of shrouds. For those who live have to eat bread. And those who die must wear shrouds. Such a combination will be proof against failure."

Delighted, the man departed and followed the rabbi's advice. But he still did not prosper and once again came running to the rabbi.

"I did what you said, holy rabbi. But now that I trade in flour and shrouds I am even worse off! Why is that?"

The rabbi was perplexed. "But surely people still live and people die?"

The merchant shrugged. "Not necessarily. Not the people in this village. The trouble is, here they don't live and they don't die. They just drag themselves around."

■

A rabbi was asked why it was that Jews always answered a question with another question. The rabbi shrugged. "Why not?"

■

A rabbi called a rich but miserly member of his congregation into his study. The man had steadfastly refused to contribute to the temple building fund. The rabbi took the man to the window and asked, "What do you see?"

"People," answered the rich man.

Then the rabbi led him to a mirror. "Now what do you see?"
"Myself."

The rabbi said, "The window is glass and the mirror is glass. But the glass in the mirror is covered with a little silver, and no sooner is a little silver added than you cease to see others and see only yourself."

■

The celebrated guest rabbi was giving an inspired address about Moses' great contributions to Judaism. Suddenly a little old man seated close to him said loudly, "Moses was a jerk!" The rabbi was amazed and annoyed and then the man said it again and again.

People started turning around.

When his talk was completed, very much annoyed at the discourtesy, the rabbi walked over to the man. "Why did you keep interrupting my sermon with such a terrible thing, that Moses was a jerk?"

The man nodded. "You heard me right, rabbi. I'm sorry that I disturbed you, but I feel very strongly about it. If Moses had turned right after they crossed the Red Sea, instead of turning left, *we* would have had the oil and they would have had the sand!"

■

In an extremely poor Russian shtetl, the rabbi was distraught because his community was so poor that they had no money to buy wine for Passover. Sick at heart, he prayed to the Lord to show him a way out of his dilemma.

The next morning he had the answer, and on Friday night, in the sparse little synagogue, he explained to his flock how they would be able to have wine for Passover. Every Friday night, in each little hut, the father of the family would pour off half a small glass from the Shabbes wine and later pour it into a large community cask that the rabbi would set up outside his door. Depositing this tiny amount, week after week until Passover, there would be enough so that each family could then draw off what was needed.

The congregation was delighted with the idea, all except Velvel, the town *schnorrer*. "*Nu*," he told his wife, "we should give up a few drops of wine we have just so he can make a big seder? No one will be any the wiser if I put in, instead, a half glass of water. In all that wine it wouldn't make any difference I can tell you."

And so, every Friday, Velvel poured in his water when no one was looking. Soon it was plain, by thumping the cask, that there would indeed be plenty of wine.

Came the appointed day and the villagers lined up, bottles and pots in hand, to get their portion. The rabbi said a brief *broche* and, taking the flask from the man at the head of the line, turned the spigot.

From it, crystal clear and untainted by the faintest tinge of color, followed a thick stream of pure cold water.

■

Nearly a hundred and fifty years ago a famous Russian rabbi was celebrated for his quick wit in always having a pertinent story no matter what subject came up. "Rabbi, tell us," one of his students asked, "how do you manage to do it?"

The rabbi smiled. "I'll explain it with a story. Once an infamous anti-Semitic Russian general was riding at the head of his troops through a small Jewish shtetl when he came to a long fence painted with more than twenty targets, colored circles.

"Marvelous to relate, in the bull's-eye of every one was a bullet hole. They never varied from dead center by so much as a fraction of an inch. The general was amazed. He had never seen such marksmanship and ordered his lieutenant to bring him the marksman.

"The local shoemaker's son, a pale and trembling youth, was shoved forward. 'Did you do that shooting?' the general asked. 'Yes, Excellency.'

"'It's astonishing! How many months have you been practicing?'

"'Never, Excellency. I never practiced. I did it the first time I ever held a gun.'

"'Then how did you hit the bull's-eye with every shot?'

"'That isn't the way I did it. I merely shot at the fence and then painted targets around every bullet hole.'"

The rabbi chuckled, "It's the same system I use. I'm never at a loss for a story to fit a subject. First, I carefully introduce a subject for which I already have the perfect story ready."

■

Izzy is astonished to learn that his aged father, Abe, has just won fourteen million dollars in the lottery. But the old man has a weak heart and Izzy is afraid that the shock will kill him. How to break it to him gently? After much thought he asks his rabbi how he should go about it.

The rabbi smiles and pats Izzy's hand. "Don't worry, my boy, I have experience in this sort of situation. Just leave it to me and ask your father to drop by."

Abe comes to the rabbi, who asks, "Abe, this is purely a hypothetical question, of course. But what would you do if you found that you had won fourteen million dollars?"

The old man says, "I'd donate a million dollars to build a sanctuary for the temple."

The rabbi drops dead.

The rabbi said to the *rebbitsin,* "We got to do something for Nudelman. He's a pillar of the congregation even though he's not an educated man. He contributes like a millionaire, which he's not, never misses a service, helps the *shammes,* drives old people to services, and is always available for a minyan. What can we do for him?"

The *rebbitsin's* face clouded, then brightened. "Why don't you make him a *haysa donda?*"

The rabbi smiled. That was it! The next day he asked Nudelman to drop by. When he did, the rabbi flashed his expensive dentistry, put his soft hand on Nudelman's shoulder, thanked him for his many services to the congregation, and appointed him official *haysa donda.*

Nudelman was both thrilled and puzzled. He lapped up the praise but didn't have the faintest idea what a *haysa donda* was or did, but was too embarrassed to ask. At home his wife didn't know. Nor did any of their friends and neighbors. Nudelman couldn't find it in any of his religious books nor in the library either.

The weekend services were approaching. Just what was he supposed to do? Finally, swallowing his pride, he went to the rabbi. "You want I should start *haysa donda*ring this *Shabbes?*"

The rabbi nodded. "Of course. We need you."

There was no way out. He had to ask. Nudelman gulped. "Rabbi, you should excuse my ignorance, but somehow I forgot what a *haysa donda* has to do."

The rabbi said, "The young kids in the religious school, especially the boys, they get restless in sabbath school and jump up and run around and bother those studying and writing.

"So you go up and down the aisles and say, 'Hey, sit down there,' and make them behave."

■

Young Rabbi Hershkowitz finally got up enough nerve to complain to the most generous member of his congregation. "Mr. Levy, I am embarrassed to bring this up, but do you always fall asleep during my sermon?"

"Look, rabbi, it's not to worry. Would I sleep if I didn't trust you?"

A wise old Russian rabbi's advice, on everything, was slavishly followed by his congregation. One morning a worried follower complained, "I invested every kopeck I had in two hundred chickens. When I went to feed them this morning, a hundred were dead. I tested their feed. It was untainted, so was their water. What, dear rabbi, should I do?"

The rabbi said, "It is plainly the work of the Lord, blessed be His name. Say a prayer. Then use the intelligence the Lord gave you and double the price of the remaining chickens and you will have lost nothing."

The villager was back next morning, wringing his hands. "Oh, rabbi, another fifty chickens died last night!"

"The ways of the Lord are often mysterious," the rabbi said. "The fifty chickens that are still living are very plainly the finest and strongest of the flock. Say another prayer of thanks to the Lord for preserving them."

It didn't help. Next morning the last fifty lay stiff in the dust. The villager tore his hair. "Now what shall I do?" he wailed.

The rabbi stroked his beard and said, "My son, I have an endless store of advice I could give you. But what use would it be to you now? You have no more chickens!"

■

After considerable "hondling" the coachman agreed to drive the rabbi to Pinsk. "But don't say I didn't warn you, it's a·rough road and a lot of it is uphill and Gretchen, my old horse, can't be hurried."

They had only gone a few miles when the road turned sharply uphill. "Gretchen will never make it with us both up that hill. So you'll have to walk up it while I guide her."

It was a long hill. The rabbi was barely reseated when the coachman said, "This next hill is even worse. But to spare Gretchen, I'll walk this time."

Shortly after, the driver said, "This next hill we're coming to is the worst of all. And I can see that Gretchen is getting really tired. So this time we'll both walk, and maybe give her a little push."

Finally, having walked nearly three-quarters of the way, they reached Pinsk. Glumly the rabbi paid the agreed-upon fare and said, "I had to come to Pinsk for the sake of my congregation. You had to come for the money. But in the name of the Master of the Universe, why did we bring Gretchen?"

■

The cantor said to the rabbi, "Is it true that a poor man has no *mazel* [luck]?"

The rabbi nodded. "Positively. If he had *mazel,* would he be poor?"

■

There aren't many really good puns in the annals of Jewish humor. But this one stayed with me: "The rabbi gets the fees, but it's the *mohel* [circumcisionist] who gets all the tips."

■

In the middle of his sermon the visiting rabbi stopped and beckoned to the *shammes.* He pointed. "That man is sound asleep. There in the third row. Wake him up."

The *shammes* shook his head. "Wake him up yourself. It's only fair. You put him to sleep."

■

Very upset, a *shlemiel* came running to his rabbi and grabbed him by the lapels. "Rabbi, rabbi, tell me what to do! Every year since we've been married my crazy wife produces a baby. Already we have ten children and not enough money to feed them. Rabbi, what shall I do?"

The rabbi thought for a moment. "Do nothing, absolutely nothing," he said.

■

A famous rabbi was so wise, so great a logician, that he could answer any question his students asked him. "Our rabbi can think his way through any situation," said one of his students. "It is true," said another, "he has a mind of unequaled power. But what if he were very tired, maybe even a little *fashnushkeyed* [drunk], would his reason still prevail over an unprecedented situation?"

And so the rabbi's loving acolytes decided to put their revered Talmud *chochem* (expert) to the test and proceeded to get him falling-down drunk. Then, while he was unconscious, they carried him to a nearby cemetery and laid him out on the grass between two tombstones—waiting to see what he would say when he awoke.

His words were a triumph of Talmudic reasoning. "If I am here, I must be dead. But if I am dead, why do I have to urinate?"

■

Persky couldn't believe his eyes. He had never been in this part of the city before. But there, before his very eyes, on Yom Kippur no less, was his rabbi slurping down oysters in Clancy's Seafood Bar. He rushed in and grabbed the rabbi's sleeve.

"Rabbi! *Gottenyu!* Eating *today!* And oysters yet!"

The nonchalant rabbi shrugged. "So what? There's an *R* in Yom Kippur, isn't there?"

■

A very poor man who lived in a one-room hovel with his wife, four children, and a mother-in-law, came to his rabbi for counsel. The crowding was impossible, he complained, and he could not afford a larger house.

The rabbi patted him consolingly. "The Lord, blessed be His name, will comfort you. Now, tell me, do you have a goat?"

"I do."

"You must bring him into the room."

"What, a goat into the house?" The rabbi nodded. The man said, "Do you realize—"

The rabbi held up his hand. "You must bring the goat into the room!"

Shaking his head, the poor man went home and brought in the goat. Three days later he ran to the rabbi, protesting loudly. "Rabbi, I brought in the goat. It's awful. Things are much worse! Help me, rabbi. Tell me what to do. I'm desperate!"

"You have chickens?" asked the rabbi.

"Three, but—"

"Bring them into your house."

"Oh, no, please, rabbi!"

"Don't argue with me, just do as I say."

The miserable man brought the chickens into his tiny house and suffered for a week before returning to the rabbi, crying, "I'm sick to my stomach. I can't stand it anymore!"

"Put the goat out," said the rabbi.

The wretched man put out the goat and returned. "It's a little better, rabbi, but you can't imagine—three dirty chickens in one room with seven people—"

"Now throw out the chickens," said the rabbi.

Next morning the man was back, smiling and happy. "Oh, rabbi, nowhere is there anyone as wise as you! Now my house is a paradise."

∎

A rabbi was seated in a Russian train when it jerked to a stop and a well-dressed young man got in and sat down across from him. The rabbi thought: This young man is not a peasant. And if he isn't, he probably comes from this district. If he does, he must be Jewish. On the other hand, why would he be going to Moscow? He's certainly not a salesman. He doesn't have a bag or a sample case with him. And a Jew doesn't go to Moscow all dressed up if it isn't for business, especially on a Friday morning. He would have to stay over the Sabbath. Unless he lives there, he wouldn't do that. And, besides, tho he's dressed nicely enough, somehow he doesn't look like a big-city person. More like a country big shot to me...Aha! Now I get it. He's not going to Moscow at all. Outside the city there's this little village, Pulyapupik. That's where he's going, calling on someone. But how many well-to-do Jewish families are there in Pulyapupik? Only two—the Chernows and the Elkins. The Elkins are a *grauber* lot. He wouldn't be calling on them. So he must be visiting the Chernows—if he isn't one of them. I don't think he is, because they're all very dark and he's blond, like a German almost.

But then, why is he visiting them? Particularly for *Shabbes*? The Chernows have only girls, so he could be a son-in-law. But if he is, which daughter did he marry? I know they're both married. Elka, I heard, married a nice university graduate, a

Cohen from Budapest. Molly's supposed to be married to a big *zhlub*. So this must be Elka's husband. Which means he's a very *frummer* Jew. But if he's from Budapest, with all the anti-Semitism there, he's not called Cohen anymore. He's changed his name, legally of course. So what's the Hungarian for Cohen? Kovacs, that's it!

But if he's changed his name, he must be a somebody, have some special status. They don't change names for nobodys. But what status—he's so young. What could it be? A doctorate from the university, I bet. He's a *doctor*, that's what he is.

The rabbi turned to the young man and smiled. "Good evening, Dr. Kovacs."

"Good evening, rabbi," answered the surprised young man, "but how do you know my name?"

The rabbi shrugged. "Oh, it's obvious."

■

A young rabbinical student was about to leave Warsaw for a congregation in Chicago. He went to his rabbi, a great Talmudic scholar, for advice on how to handle his American congregation, particularly the young boys in the *yeshiva* (Talmudic academy). The sage instructed him for two hours in all the niceties of teaching and exactly how he should conduct himself—how to instruct the young Americans thirsting for knowledge.

Finally, the old man rose and placed his hand on the student's head for a final *broche*.

"You will do well, my son, if you remember all I have told you. Plus one other area of instruction closest to the hearts of all the *yeshiva buchers*—learn to play baseball!"

■

"Rabbi, why did God create *goyim*?"
"In his wisdom He knew *somebody* had to buy retail."

■

A rabbi and a Methodist minister happened to be seated next to each other on an airliner. A pretty young stewardess came down the aisle and asked, "Would you care for a cocktail?"

"Why, yes," the rabbi said, "I'll have a martini, extra dry."

"Thank you, sir. And you, reverend?"

He scowled. "Before I touch strong drink, young lady, I'd just as soon commit adultery."

"Oh, miss," the rabbi said. "I didn't know there was a choice. As long as there is, I'll have what he's having."

■

A Westchester family wanted a rabbi to bless their new Mercedes and called the Orthodox rabbi.

"How can I do that," he replied. "I don't even know what a Mercedes is."

They called a Conservative rabbi. "Rabbi, will you make a *broche* over our new Mercedes?"

He hemmed and hawed. "I'm sorry, but I don't know if I can or not."

Finally they called a Reform rabbi. "Rabbi, would you make a *broche* over our Mercedes?"

"Sure," he said, "but what's a *broche?*"

■

Unable to resist the urge, early one Yom Kippur morning, a fanatical Reform rabbi sneaked out of his house and went for a quick nine holes before the long day's services. An invisible angel flying by saw him and immediately notified God.

God caused a mighty wind to take the ball over three hundred yards directly from the tee for a miraculous, unbelievable hole-in-one.

The angel was mystified. "O Master of the Universe," he protested, "this you call a punishment?"

"The greatest," answered God with a smile. "Whom can he tell?"

■

Walking down the street in Haifa with a disciple on the Sabbath, a rabbi sees a fifty-shekel note fall from his pocket. The disciple is aghast. "Rabbi, how can you violate the commandment against carrying money on *Shabbes?*"

The rabbi's eyes opened widely in wonderment as he bent to pick up the cash. "Oh, this? You call this money?"

■

A wealthy cynic came to visit a rabbi famous for his wonder working. "*Sholem aleichem,* rabbi," he said and handed him a ten-dollar bill.

The rabbi smilingly accepted the gift and said, "Peace be unto you, too. Have you come to see me on some personal matter—something about your wife or children?"

"No, rabbi," the man said, taking another ten-dollar bill from his wallet and handing it to him. "Nothing like that, I'm not married."

"Then maybe you have come to inquire about some religious matter, some fine points in the interpretation of Jewish law?"

"No, rabbi, I can't even read Hebrew. Not that."

"Then you have come to ask me to bless your business?"

"No, rabbi," the man answered. "I'm enjoying a very good year." And he handed over another ten-dollar bill. "I only hope every year will be as good."

The rabbi looked perplexed. "My friend, I don't understand. You obviously came here for something. What is it you wish?"

The man handed him another ten dollars. "I was curious to see how long a man could go on accepting money for nothing."

■

A rabbi was asked by one of his poor flock what God thought of money. The old man fingered his beard and then said, "What does He think of *gelt*? Ha! Just look at the people he gives it to."

■

A man says to a rabbi, "I don't know how you can get by with such a small congregation. Tell me the truth, how much do they pay you a week?"

The rabbi said, "Sometimes I take in as much as forty, fifty dollars a week."

The man said, "How can you live on that?"

The rabbi shrugged. "If I wasn't very religious and didn't fast three days a week, I'd starve to death."

■

Two sad-faced Talmudic students made an embarrassed confession to their rabbi. "Rabbi, we have sinned."

"Sinned? What sin?"

"We looked upon a woman with lust."

The holy man recoiled. "That is a serious transgression. You must atone immediately."

"Tell us, rabbi," they said in unison, "how can we atone?"

"If you seriously seek penance, I direct you to each put a handful of dried peas into your shoes. Walk about on them for ten days. That should teach you not to sin again. Every step will remind you."

The students went home and followed the rabbi's order. A few days later they met on the temple steps. One hobbled painfully but the other walked easily with a springy step.

"So you disobeyed the rabbi," his friend accused him. "I see you did not put the peas into your shoes as he ordered."

"You are wrong," his companion said, smiling. "I simply cooked them first."

■

The Jewish father had tears in his eyes. "Rabbi," he cried, "tell me what to do. Something terrible has happened. My son wants to marry a *shiksa!*"

The rabbi said, "You think *you* have trouble! Next to me that's nothing. *My son* not only wants to marry a gentile girl, but he wants to be baptized! And here I am, the leader of the community, looked up to as an example. I am disgraced!"

There was silence. Then the Jew asked, "If everyone comes to you with their problems, rabbi, whom do you turn to with yours?"

"What can I do? I turn to God."

"So what did God tell you?"

"God said to me, '*Your* son?...Look at mine.'"

■

Rabbi Brownstein was a famous speaker, of such eloquence that he could move an audience to laughter or tears at will. He was called to deliver the eulogy at the funeral of a very rich man. He leaned forward at the podium and turned on all his power.

He elaborated on the many good works and charities of the deceased: his generosity to the synagogue, to the poor and to indigent students; his benevolence to hospitals and to homes for the aged; on the nobility of his character and the tragedy of his demise at so early an age.

Yet his listeners were unmoved. There was not a sob or sniffle, not even from members of the immediate family. Rabbi Brownstein felt defeated.

On the way home from the funeral one of his friends said to him, "They were certainly a cold lot. You were magnificent, but there wasn't even one tear from any of the mourners. I don't understand it."

The rabbi sighed. "My job is only to turn on the faucet. Is it my fault if nothing comes out?"

4 A Taste of Midrash

Midrash is a complicated, highly particularized analysis and interpretation of the Hebrew Bible (the Torah). It is an attempt to explain further and fill in the details of the sparsely written biblical stories—so that their meanings are fully understood in all ages by all kinds of people.

In writing midrash, rabbis often allowed their imaginations to run riot with what they considered convincing minutiae (that probably would have astounded the original biblical authors!).

After the destruction of Solomon's Temple, there was an endless flow of such instructional preaching. The skills of the authors varied widely, but their total output was tremendous. From the fourth century A.D. on, these preachings were all written down, so that today there are more than a hundred books of midrash!

Following are some examples of modern midrash in parody form. Humorous parodies were not frowned upon. Strangely, Jews took no offense. They firmly believed the gospel truth of the original stories as handed down in the Torah, while cackling appreciatively over broad parodies.

Just a few seasons back, Bill Cosby panicked millions of viewers with two midrash routines that depicted Noah having some fairly sassy dialogue with God.

Here are some modern examples of humorous midrash. The first is a parody on what happened when the Israelites found no transport waiting when they arrived at the Red Sea with

Pharaoh's chariots in hot pursuit. With minor variations, the following whimsy is making the rounds today—its author unknown but certainly not unappreciated.

■   ■   ■

Led by the tall, commanding figure of Moses, the Israelites are fleeing madly across the burning desert in clouds of Technicolor dust. Scant minutes behind and rapidly overtaking them, another, larger cloud of dust is rising from the pursuing Egyptians.

At the shore Moses raises his staff and yells, "Schwartz! Schwartz! Where the devil are the boats I ordered?"

Breathless, red-faced, and pouring sweat, up dashes his faithful Director of Public Relations.

"Dammit, where are the boats?"

"The wha-a-at?"

"The boats to carry us across the Red Sea, you offspring of a diseased camel!"

Schwartz is now sweating bullets, his face red as sunset. "Oh, golly, boss, what with everything else on my list, the human interest stories, the interviews and the release for the *Daily Pyramid,* I just didn't get around to it. I forgot!"

"You forgot, you thrice-damned idiot! *You forgot!* That cloud of dust is Pharaoh's army, you fermented crock of mule dung. Now what am I supposed to do—explain this to God? Get Him to roll back the waters when I raise my staff, so we can walk across on dry land? And then have him roll the waters back and drown the Egyptians coming after us? Do you think—"

Schwartz interrupted, falling to his knees and grabbing the hem of Moses' robe, his eyes shining. "Boss, you pull that off and I'll guarantee you at least two pages in the Old Testament!"

This next example of modern midrash is a one-act comedy about Isaac and Abraham and what *really* happened on Mount Moriah. It was actually produced before a Bible study class in Deerfield, Illinois, on August 8, 1990.

The Straight Scoop About Abraham and Isaac
or

Why the Ram Got Stuck Instead of the Kid

Our scene opens in Abraham's tent on the edge of the desert just at daybreak.

(sound of heavy snoring)

Sarah: Up, up, you two paskudnyaks. Get yourselves dressed, you've got a big trip ahead of you.

Abraham: *(Groaning)* Already? The sun isn't even up.

Isaac: Ah, Ma. I don't want to go to school today!

Sarah: You're not going to school, today, *draykop*, remember? You're going to the mountains. Your father has a surprise there for you. I'm making lunch already, so hurry up.

Abraham: Good Lord, I'm coming. Be right with you.
(sound of donkeys braying—hee-haw, hee-haw)

Abraham:	Hop to it, Isaac, and saddle up those asses. Better clean out the stable too, while you're at it. And then be sure to wash your hands before you come to the table. *(clatter of dishes, table silver)*
Sarah:	*Ess, ess,* you've got a long trip ahead of you. You shouldn't ride on an empty stomach!
Isaac:	Aw, Ma, *manna* again!
Sarah:	What do you expect, oat bran? They haven't invented it yet. Put milk and honey on it, it'll taste better.
Abraham:	Anybody seen my big knife? You can't put a damned thing down in this tent but it disappears!
Sarah:	What do you need a butcher knife for? Better you should take the ax for firewood. It gets cold there in the mountains. You don't need the knife.
Abraham:	Don't give me any arguments. When I say I need the knife, *I need the knife!* You been chopping liver with it again? Where is it?
Sarah:	Don't make such a *gonsa* deal. Look out by the chopping block. I was cleaning there a chicken. Be sure you wipe it off good. Use sand, it cleans pretty good but I'll sure be glad when they invent steel wool. *(sound of departure—donkeys braying, hooves clip-clopping, fading away)*
Sarah:	*(Yelling after them)* Abe, don't forget, you get a chance, bring me back a nice, fat ram. The holidays are coming. *(sounds of travel—donkeys braying, the clip-clop of hooves)*
Isaac:	Hey, Pa. We nearly there yet? We been riding three days already. What are we going to do when we get to Mount Moriah anyway—fish? Hunt?
Abraham:	*(Long sigh)* Questions, questions, always with the questions. Did I ever steer you wrong yet? When we get to Mount Moriah, you'll see. It'll be just like old times, just you and me. We'll leave the servants down with the asses.

(sound of footsteps and heavy breathing)

Isaac: Whew, this is some shlep! Do we have to go all the way to the top? Especially with all this firewood. I'm sweating—you should excuse the expression— like a pig. What do we need so much wood for? We going to start a forest fire, or what?

Abraham: Again with the questions! But, all right, I'll tell you. I'm going to make a burnt offering to the Lord. So first we have to build an altar on which to put it. Then we pile the wood all around. There, you can put your load down, right over there.

(sound of knocking, hammering)

Isaac: Okay, we got the altar. Swell. But what's cooking? We didn't bring a sheep or a goat or anything. I think you're slipping, Pop. *What* are we going to sacrifice?

Abraham: You mean what am *I* going to sacrifice. I am going to sacrifice my dearest possession, the child of my old age. YOU! You, Isaac.

Isaac: *(Yelling)* ARE YOU NUTS! Where'd you ever get that *meshuggeneh* idea? You're crazy! That's murder! You kill me and you'll louse up the whole course of Jewish history. Matter of fact, without me there won't *be* any Jewish history. Because you're too old to have any more kids. So cool it, Pop!

Abraham: *(Sobbing)* Do you think I *want* to do this? But the Lord has asked and I have faith in the Lord. So come over here and lie down so I can get this over with. Believe me, this is going to hurt me more than it hurts you.

Isaac: The hell it is! Take a good look at that knife and tell me you believe it. *Don't do it!* If God really asked you to sacrifice me, then He got His signals crossed. Or maybe He just didn't think it through. How you gonna have any Judaism without any Jews? He gotta come up with a better deal!

(sound of bushes rustling and sheep baaaaing)

Abraham:	Look, Isaac, there's a ram caught in the thicket!
Isaac:	See, God sent you a replacement for me! He must have thought it over. Maybe He heard what I said. God's still got all His marbles, thank God!
Abraham:	How can we be sure it was the Lord who sent us this ram?
Isaac:	You know anybody else trying to herd sheep in the woods on top of a mountain?
Abraham:	Oh praised be the Lord! But—but—how did the ram get here?
Isaac:	I don't care if he got dropped from a helicopter— that's an old Greek word, I'll explain it later. The important thing is that the ram is here. Help me grab him before he breaks free. Or you'll be after me with the God-damned knife again.
Abraham:	Praised be the Lord! How wondrous are His works!
Isaac:	And he's practical, too. After we roast that ram we'll have enough mutton for a party. Which is a lot more than you would have gòtten out of me!
Abraham:	I can't wait to tell your mother about this. She'll never believe it.
Isaac:	Sure she will. She'll believe anything. So will millions of others. We'll go down in history!
Abraham:	And now I won't have to buy her that ram she asked for, and this one'll be all cooked besides. Praised be the Lord!
	(fadeout of hooves clopping and donkey bells tinkling)

Midrash need not be confined to words alone. There have been many drawings and cartoons lampooning the sacred biblical tales. None, to my mind, more screamingly funny than Shel Silverstein's savage six panels entitled: "The Twenty Commandments"—included in his collection *Different Dances.*

Completely unlike Charleton Heston's majestic Moses, here the great leader is depicted as a skinny, naked, bald, wild-whiskered little old man—the epitome of weakness and insignificance.

The great hand of God pokes down through the heavens and deposits a huge double-stone tablet—as tall as Moses and more than twice as wide.

Feeble little Moses unsuccessfully attempts to lift the tablet. From somewhere he takes a mallet and chisel and splits the tablet into two equal parts—with ten Commandments on each half. He then staggers off down Mount Sinai, painfully lugging the commandments we know, leaving the others behind. In case you're curious about what they *didn't* teach you in Sunday School, here they are:

Thou shalt not compromise.
Thou shalt not judge.
Thou shalt not seek rewards.
Thou shalt not follow leaders.
Remember every day to keep it holy.
Honor thy children.
Mind thine own business.
Thou shalt not destroy the body before its time.
Thou shalt not waste thy time.
Thou shalt not lay guilt upon the head of thy neighbor.

The Logic of Chelm

The folklore of most people includes some particular location where the populace is especially foolish, impractical, naïve, or just plain dim-witted. In England such a place was Gotham; in Greece, Abdera; in Holland, Kampen; in Italy, Cuneo; and in Germany, Schildberg. Stories about Schildberg were translated into Yiddish as early as 1597.

These towns were all supposedly inhabited by simpletons, halfwits, and fools. And of course it provided the tellers of tales about them great satisfaction by showing their own superiority.

Such a town was Chelm (pronounced *Khelm,* like clearing one's throat). Although much has been written about it, it is still unclear how Chelm earned its reputation for idiotic reasoning and outlandish non sequiturs.

We Americans have (or had, at least) our own targets of ridicule—Brooklyn, N.Y.... where the "woims sqoim in poifect soicles," and, for different reasons, Peoria, Illinois. Peorians, slow on the uptake, had to have everything oversimplified and/or morally spotless. Hence the producer's query about anything new: "But how will it play in Peoria?"

A presumed city of incredible nincompoops, Chelm, as used in Yiddish fable, is a mythical place. Actually, there were two Chelms—one forty miles east of Lublin in Poland and another directly east of Tarnow.

The natives of mythological Chelm seriously considered themselves scholars and logicians. To European Jews it was the home of befuddled thinkers and reasoners, sarcastically referred to as "the wise men of Chelm." According to one fable, the concentration of boobs in Chelm was due to a mishap in God's delivery system. He had dispatched an angel with two sacks—one filled with wise souls and one full of foolish ones. The purpose was to have them distributed equally in many communities. But, unfortunately, while the angel was flapping his wings over Chelm, he was flying too low and one of the sacks ripped open on a mountaintop so that all the fools fell into Chelm.

■ ■ ■

One day the wise men of Chelm were arguing about which was more important to mankind: the sun or the moon? The town was evenly divided into two violently opposed groups, each headed by its own rabbi. Finally, the rabbis put the question to the leading sage, whom all revered. He pondered the matter for days and then called the rabbis to him.

He ruled: The moon was, of course, more important than the sun because it came out in the dark so that men could see. The sun, on the other hand, came out in the bright daylight when all could see plainly without it.

■

A rabbi from Chelm once visited the prison where all the inmates but one insisted that they were innocent and had been wrongly jailed. The rabbi called his wise men together and insisted that the town build another jail—so that they would have one for the innocent and one for the guilty.

■

A wise man of Chelm called all the merchants together for the purpose of revising their credit system. Said he: "In this crazy world the rich, who have plenty of money, buy on credit. But the poor, who have no credit, have to pay cash. It should be the other way round. The rich, having money, should have to pay cash. The poor who have no money should get credit. This was only fair."

The storekeeper objected. "If I give credit to the poor I would soon become poor myself!"

"Good!" said the wise man, "then you'll be able to buy on credit too!"

A local Chelm comedian once proposed a riddle that no one could answer: "What's purple, hangs on the wall, and whistles?" No one could solve it so they gave up and asked for the answer.

Said the jokester, "A herring!"

"A herring?" a man said. "A herring isn't purple!"

"*Nu*," said the jokester, "*this* herring was painted purple."

"But hanging on a wall? Herrings don't hang on walls!"

"Fooled you. *This* herring was hung on the wall."

Someone else shouted, "But a herring doesn't whistle!"

"All right, so I exaggerated a little."

■

In Chelm the inhabitants go to the dentist to have wisdom teeth put in.

■

Zolman, a Chelm dairyman, is walking to his cow shed one morning when a stranger runs over to him and slaps him in the face. "That's for you, Mendel," the stranger yells.

After recovering from the shock, Zolman begins to laugh.

"What are you laughing at?" the stranger asks. "Do you want me to hit you again?"

"No, please, no," says Zolman. "It's just that the joke's on you—I'm not Mendel!"

■

One of Chelm's wise men came to the rabbi. "I have a question," he said. "Why is it that if you drop a slice of bread with butter on it that it always lands with the buttered side down?"

"I don't know that that's true," said the rabbi. "Let's try it and see." He buttered a slice of bread and dropped it. But the buttered side was facing up.

"*Nu*," said the rabbi, "you obviously are working from a false premise."

"But, rabbi," the wise man answered, "you obviously buttered the wrong side."

■

Two wise men of Chelm were taking a walk when it suddenly began to rain—a downpour. "Quick, open your umbrella," said one.

"It won't help," his friend said, "my umbrella is full of holes."

"Then why did you bring it?"

"I didn't think it would rain," he said.

In the interests of economy, saving time and fuel, the wise men of Chelm passed a resolution requiring all poultrymen to feed their hens hot water so that they would lay boiled eggs.

■

A visitor asked one of Chelm's wise men why they built the railway station three miles from Chelm. The man answered, "We all thought it was a good thing to have it near the trains."

■

"Heat," explained a wise man of Chelm to another, "makes things expand and cold makes them contract."

"Prove it to me," his fellow citizen said. "Where is it written?"

"The proof is ever before you," said his companion. "How else do you account for the longer days in summer and the shorter ones in winter?"

■

A distraught woman brought her case before the ruling committee of Chelm. "O masters," she wept, "six months ago my husband went out for a *challah* [white loaf] and never came back. What should I do?"

The committee told her to return the next day. And she did.

"Peace unto you," said the committee chairman, "my associates and I have considered every aspect of your case. Do not wait any longer. Send one of the children out for another bread."

6

Luftmenshen

Perhaps it would be as well to tell a story about a *luftmensh* before trying to define one. It's a classic and goes like this:

■ ■ ■

Farfelman, *luftmensh* extraordinaire, buttonholes his old friend, Lipsky, on busy Canal Street in New York City. He is all ingratiating smiles and puts his hands on his friend's shoulders.

"*Landsman,* you surely got luck. You almost missed out. I tried to get you on the phone earlier. Have I got a bargain for you, an offer you can't refuse: a genuine Barnum and Bailey specially trained elephant. He's young, beautiful, in good health—extra-large size. And for you only, just one thousand dollars."

Lipsky's eyes widened; he recoiled. "A what? Are you crazy or something? What the hell would I do with an elephant?"

Farfelman's smile widened. He tightened his grip on his friend's shoulders. "Old buddy, I see you don't understand. This is the genuine article. Not some shrimpy old Indian elephant, but an A-number one *African* elephant with the big ears!"

Lipsky's voice rose. "You're positively crazy! You know I live in a three-room apartment. What are you hocking me with *elephants!*"

Farfelman went right on. "And tusks like you never saw, big, heavy, not a nick out of them—solid ivory."

Now Lipsky screeched, "Enough already. Stop the *mishegoss!* I'm on the fourth floor of a walkup. Where could I park this thing?"

Farfelman sighed. "You certainly drive a hard bargain. You're a tough man. But, all right, I'll tell you what I'm going to do. For only two hundred and fifty dollars extra, I'll throw in a baby elephant, a darling little thing. Both for twelve hundred and fifty dollars."

Lipsky smiled and rubbed his hands together. "Now, *now* you're talking."

There is no concise, all-encompassing definition of a *luftmensh*. Probably because he was so many things. But he was always impractical. Strictly a European Jew, he was usually an inhabitant of some East European ghetto who was perforce a dreamer of impossible schemes, imaginative because of desperation.

Ghetto life offered a Jew few pathways to success. Most ways of making a living, open to gentiles, were closed to him. So the *luftmensh* tried to invent new paths. Of course, there were a great many Jewish laborers, merchants, dairymen, teachers, artisans, and peddlers. But there were usually more Jews than jobs. Consequently many a hard-pressed Jew strove to wring a few kopecks from esoteric enterprises—goods and services that no one wanted and frequently didn't exist. These "businesses" existed only in the *luftmensh's* busy imagination.

A Dictionary of Yiddish Slang and Idioms by Fred Kogos (Citadel Press) defines a *luftmensh* as "person who has no business, trade, calling, nor income and is forced to live by improvisation, drawing his livelihood 'from the air.'" Which brings us back to the elephant pitchman and his pigeon. Another, but not exclusively Jewish, trait is illustrated by the above tale: man's irresistible susceptibility to a bargain.

In Kogo's definition there is more than a faint implication that a *luftmensh* was inherently lazy, unwilling to work. Not so. Sometimes his efforts were prodigious. All he lacked was *mazel* (luck).

There is the case of perhaps the supreme *luftmensh* of all time, one Leone da Modena, an energetic sixteenth-century Venetian Jew who claimed to be engaged in all the following occupations:

> Rabbi
> Cantor
> Preacher

Rabbinical judge
Hebrew teacher
   (to Jews and Gentiles)
Italian playwright
Hebrew poet
Theatrical producer
Ghost writer
Music teacher
Shadchen
Commercial agent
Translator
Printer
Proofreader
Writer of legal documents
Composer of epitaphs for Jewish tombstones
Seller of charms and talismans
Secretary of charitable and other Jewish societies

There is no record of his having died rich.

Consider the *Shnorrer*

A vital figure in the typical shtetl, the *shnorrer* is not only difficult to define (we have four complicated definitions before us) but *shnorrer* itself is spelled three different ways: *schnorrer, shnorer,* and *shnorrer,* which we will use here.

Leo Rosten says he is:

1. A beggar, a panhandler, a moocher.
2. A cheapskate, a chiseler.
3. A bum, a drifter.
4. A compulsive bargain hunter and bargainer.
5. An impudent indigent.

Fred Kogos, an equally respected scholar, says a *shnorrer* is:

A beggar who makes pretensions to respectability, sponger, chiseler, moocher, a parasite, but always with brass and resourcefulness in getting money from others as though it were his right.

Every European Jewish community had at least one *shnorrer* and often a platoon of them. He was no ordinary panhandler. He never fawned or whined, but regarded himself as a craftsman, a supreme technician in the delicate art of getting something for nothing. He never begged—he demanded, a consummate expert in wheedling and needling. Bold, fresh, often insulting, his attitude and methods were cultivatedly outrageous. The *shnorrer* haggled over the amounts offered, berating those who underpaid or refused to give what was demanded.

Shnorrers considered themselves unofficial agents of God, who bade all Jews to fulfill their obligations of helping the poor and unfortunate, and thus earn *mitzvahs* (blessings).

Though often uneducated, he was neither a fool nor a simpleton. Frequently he *was* well-read, was a regular in the synagogue, and participated in theological discussion with his benefactors, even quoting from the Talmud to extract contributions. Herewith the *shnorrer* in action:

■ ■ ■

Mrs. Chernow's heart bled for the hungry *shnorrer* at her door. She invited him in and fed him royally: roast chicken, kugel, wine, and both black bread and challah. He devoured everything but the black bread. "Your *challah* is wonderful," he said. "You got maybe a few more slices?"

"Look, mister," Mrs. Chernow said, "we have plenty of black bread, but *challah* is very expensive.

"I know," the *shnorrer* said, "but believe me, it's worth it."

■

A *shnorrer* once wangled his way in to see the mighty Baron Rothschild by writing that he had a surefire way for the Baron to make a half million rubles.

"So let's hear your great idea," said the doubting Rothschild.

"It's very simple and absolutely foolproof," answered the *shnorrer*. "Everyone knows that when your daughter gets married you're going to give her a dowry of a million rubles."

"*Nu?* So what?"

"So I've come to tell you that I'll marry her for half that amount!"

■

The local *shnorrer* comes to Mandelbaum for his monthly handout. A distraught-looking Mandelbaum comes to the door himself, no servant. The *shnorrer* asks, "What's the matter, something wrong?"

"I've gone bankrupt, haven't you heard?"

"Of course I've heard."

"Then what do you want from me?"

"The same as everyone else, ten cents on the dollar."

■

A *shnorrer* knocked on the door of a very humble cottage, part of his weekly rounds. The *baleboosteh* (housewife) wrung her hands in anguish. "I haven't a kopeck in the house," she apologized. "Come back tomorrow."

"What do you mean 'tomorrow'?" The *shnorrer* wagged a

menacing finger under her nose. "Never let this happen again. I've already lost a fortune extending credit."

■

An accosted man said to the *shnorrer,* "Why should I give you a kopeck? Go out and work. You've got the arms and legs of a dray horse!"

"So!" sneered the *shnorrer,* "for your lousy kopeck I'm supposed to cut off my limbs?"

■

At 6:00 in the morning a *shnorrer* banged on the door of a rich man's house. The awakened man looked out of the second story.

"What do you mean waking me up so early? How dare you!"

"Listen, mister," said the *shnorrer,* "I don't tell you how to run your business. So don't tell me how to run mine."

■

The *shnorrer* stopped a prosperous-looking man. "I'm not asking for anything terrific, maybe a groschen?"

The man's face froze. "I don't hand out money on the street!"

"So what am I supposed to do," the *shnorrer* asked, "open an office?"

■

A *shnorrer* said to the shtetl's richest citizen, "Don't look so hard at me. I didn't come here to beg. I'm here to make a bet with you."

"You want to bet? About what?"

"I'll bet you ten rubles I can get something you can't!"

The big shot smiled and slapped ten rubles on his desk. "It's a bet," he said.

The *shnorrer* swept them into his gaping pocket. "I," he said, "can get a certificate showing I am a pauper."

■

An advertising executive gave a dime every day to the *shnorrer* stationed outside his office building, boxes of pencils in a little tray suspended from the beggar's neck. The executive never took a pencil. One day the man dropped his usual dime and headed into the building when he felt a light tap on his shoulder. It was the *shnorrer.* "Mister, I hate to do this, but I've had to raise my prices. A pencil now costs a quarter."

■

An *alrightnik* in a vicuña coat gave a *shnorrer* a nickel and asked, "How did a strong, healthy young man like you become a panhandler?"

"Because I was just like you," the *shnorrer* answered, "always giving away large sums of money."

■

In a wealthy residential district on Chicago's Gold Coast, a *shnorrer* stood outside a wealthy synagogue extending his hat. One Sabbath he failed to appear. Mrs. Goldblatt, who already had her fistful of small change ready, turned to her husband. "I hope he's not sick," she said.

Her husband sniffed. "That *shnorrer?* He's healthy as a horse. Probably in Florida this time of year."

■

Pinsky, an insolent little *shnorrer* of Vilna, had for years depended on the generosity of Gompert, the wealthiest man in the community. For no visible reason he had taken a liking to the little sharper and every New Year's would give Pinsky a little bag of five hundred rubles. On this particular holiday, however, he gave him only two hundred and fifty.

"What are you trying to get away with?" the audacious little *shnorrer* demanded. "This is only half what you owe me!"

The rich man apologized. "I'm sorry, Pinsky, but it's been a very bad year and I have to cut expenses. My son married an actress, a woman of very expensive tastes, and I am paying all the bills."

Pinsky shouted in anger, "Some *chutzpah!* If he wants to support an actress, let him. But he can't do it with my money."

■

The *shnorrer* walked into Bernstein's Bar, asked for a glass of water, drank it, and walked out. Next day he did the same thing. And the next. The fourth time the bartender said, "Hey, you, wait a minute. You come in here, ask for a glass of water, drink it, and walk out...."

"What do you want me to do," interrupted the *shnorrer*, "stagger?"

■

The *shnorrer* was brought before the rabbi, charged with stealing a coat. The rabbi peered at him closely then asked, "Wasn't it just three years ago that you were brought before me also charged with stealing a coat?"

"Yes," said the *shnorrer*, "how long do you think a coat lasts?"

8

The *Tsouris of Shadchens* With Some Smiles From the Shtetl

Very often the *shadchen* (professional matchmaker and marriage broker) had a terrible time making a match. All the females in his territory were not young or pretty or rich—or even healthy. Many were not very appetizing altogether, and as it was strictly the man's choice in those unenlightened days, the poor broker had a tough time earning his few rubles. He was only paid if a marriage resulted from his efforts; near misses didn't count.

His resourcefulness and imagination were frequently taxed to the limit, as these few tales will illustrate.

■ ■ ■

A certain *shadchen* in Pinsk took his eager young prospective bridegroom to meet a young (?) woman. The young man took a quick look, his eyes widened, and he turned and attempted to run out the door. The *shadchen* grabbed his coattail.

"So what's the matter?" he asked.

The young man whispered, but in a fury. "You lied to me! You said she was young. She'll never see forty again! You told me she was beautiful. She looks like the back of a cow! You said she had a nice figure—and she's fat enough for two girls! You said—"

The shadchen interrupted, "You don't have to whisper," soothed the matchmaker, "she also doesn't hear so good."

■

A young man patiently sat and listened to a *shadchen* rave about a young woman he had just introduced. The young man sneered. "But didn't you leave out something?"

"Of course not. What?"

"She limps!"

"Only when she walks," explained the *shadchen*.

■

A prospective groom shook an impassioned finger under his *shadchen*'s nose. He scowled. "You lied to me!"

"I lied?" the insulted *shadchen* protested. "How? She's pretty, isn't she? Intelligent? Rich? What more do you want?"

"Sure, sure," said the young man. "But you said she came from a famous family and that her father is dead. Well, that's a damned lie! I just found out that he's been in jail for the past five years!"

The *shadchen* shrugged. "So? *That* you call living?"

After the *shadchen's* fevered pitch, the young man could hardly wait to see his blind date. "A regular picture!" the *shadchen* had assured him.

But when he saw the *shadchen* next day the young man was furious. "A 'regular picture,'" he mimicked. "She's cockeyed, her big nose is crooked. And when she tries to smile—*oy!* One side of her mouth goes down!"

"Hold on just a minute," said the *shadchen*. "Is it my fault you don't like Picasso?"

■

The *shadchen* was reassuring his client about a prospective bride's family. "Their house may not seem so grand, but the people got money. Look at the expensive furnishings, the fine china, the silverware. Just feel this genuine Oriental—"

"Ha," interrupted the suspicious potential groom. "To make on me a good impression they could have borrowed all these things."

"*Borrowed?*" ridiculed the *shadchen*. "Borrowed? Who would lend anything to such paupers!"

9

Juice From the Big Apple

Manhattan—New York, N.Y., the Big Apple! (To be precise we have to exclude Brooklyn, Bronx, Queens, and Richmond.) Yet their inhabitants are proud to be considered part of Greater New York, never offended when you call them New Yorkers. The glamour rubs off—and besides, many of them work in the Big Apple even if they don't sleep there.

In Manhattan there is more, and more concentrated, *everything* that goes into producing HUMOR—Jewish or goyish: more talented writers; publishers; actors; stand-up comedians; gag men; radio and TV producers; cassette, record, and tape makers; and so on, than anywhere else—including its pale competitor, Hollywood, and all stops in between.

The Big Apple is the sweetest, juiciest *headquarters for every stripe of laugh-producer.*

It is an incredible concentration of creativity, encompassing the great names that draw the crowds as well as those who will become great in the near future. They mature fast in the Big Apple or disappear quickly.

Aloud, or only in their secret hearts, they all consider the Big Apple to be their spiritual home—even while they are *temporarily* raking in a fat living on the opposite coast or elsewhere.

Here, then, is some Big Apple concentrate, Jewish laughs from the capital of creativity—the incomparable fountainhead of Jewish jokes—New York, New York.

■　■　■

Ginsburg had been enjoying the chicken soup in Ratner's famous East Side restaurant for years. He was such a regular that the waiter set down a steaming bowl in front of him unasked. But this night Ginsburg merely glared at it and snapped his fingers for the waiter.

"Taste this soup!" he demanded.

The waiter was puzzled. "For what? It's just like always. It's wonderful. I don't have to taste it. Eat it and enjoy."

Ginsburg banged his fist on the table. *"Taste this soup!"* he demanded. *"Right now!"*

The waiter shrugged. "All right, all right, don't excite yourself. If it makes you happy I'll taste it. But where's the spoon?"

"Aha!" cried Ginsburg.

■

A straphanger in a New York subway swayed over a little old woman who squinted up at him steadily. Finally she tapped his knee. "Pardon my curiosity," she said, "but are you Jewish?"

"No, madam, I'm not."

Two minutes later she shook the paper he was trying to read. "You should excuse me, but you're *sure* you're not Jewish?"

"Absolutely," the man answered.

The woman was still not convinced. She pulled on his paper. "Come on, tell me the truth, are you absolutely sure you're not Jewish, hah?"

"All right, all right," the man said, "You got me. You win. I'm Jewish."

"That's funny," said the woman. "You sure don't *look* Jewish."

■

The latest in New York child psychology was practiced by Pamela Weinstein, whose ten-year-old, Gregory, had been an especial pain in the butt, disrupting his entire class with his wisecracks.

She wrote his teacher, "If Gregory is a bad boy, don't slap him—he's very sensitive. The next time he cuts up, slap the boy *next* to him, hard. Gregory is very quick. He'll get the idea."

■

Two psychiatrists were in the elevator going home at the end of a long day. The younger man looked beat, haggard, and worn. The older man looked as though he had just come fresh from a night's rest.

The younger one said, "I don't know how you do it. You've got a case load bigger than mine and yet you look like you could put in another day. Nothing seems to bother you, while my patients are driving me crazy. All day they keep hammering at me with all their problems until I'm exhausted. Isn't it just the same with your patients? Don't you get weary and depressed sitting there all day listening to them?"

"Ahhhh," said the older doctor, "who listens?"

■

Moishe "Machine Gun" Koplowitz, a hit man for a notorious East Side Jewish gang, got caught in a crossfire during a gang shootout and was severely wounded. Doubled over and in agony, he managed to drag himself away and, finally, crawl four blocks to his mother's flat.

Dripping blood, he hauled himself up the stairs to her door and banged on it with his last strength.

"Ma, Ma, it's me, Moishe. I'm hurt bad!"

"Sit down and eat," his mother said. "Later we'll talk."

■

Two Jews meet in front of Radio City Music Hall. They shake hands. One asks, "Harry, what's with you? You still in show business?"

"N-n-no. I just got turned down for a g-g-good j-j-job announcing at International Broadcasting. The b-b-bastards!"

"How come?"

"The s-s-station manager was a d-d-damned anti-Semite!"

■

Four salesmen on a Long Island commuter train got a deck of cards from the conductor and began to play cards.

"My name's Cowlan," said one man.

"I'm Curtis," said the second salesman.

"Carleton," the third said.

"Also Cohen," added the fourth.

■

A recent Jewish immigrant from Poland saw a man reading the Yiddish paper on a park bench, on the Sabbath, and smoking a cigar.

"America, America," he said in wonder. "Here even the *goyim* can read Yiddish."

■

Bromberg lost his wallet at a big UJA testimonial dinner. He stood at the microphone and announced, "Ladies and gentlemen, I've lost my wallet with five hundred dollars in it. Whoever finds it will get a fifty-dollar reward."

A stranger pushed Bromberg away from the mike. "I'll give seventy-five!" he said.

■

Malkowitz, a clothing manufacturer, returned from a trip to Rome. His partner asked if he enjoyed the vacation.

"Wonderful, wonderful, there's no place like it."

"By any chance did you get to see the Pope?"

"Of course I saw the Pope, as near to him as you are."

"So, how was he?"

"I figure a forty-two long."

■

An elderly Jew goes into Tiffany's to buy his wife a present. He sees a magnificent sterling-silver crucifix, picks it up, and hefts it.

"Nice," he says. "Nice. What do you want for it?"

"That's eight hundred dollars, sir," answers the clerk.

"Mmm," says the man, "and how much without the acrobat?"

■

Hannah Goldstone took her precious three-year-old grandson to Jones Beach. All dressed up in his darling little sailor suit and hat, he squatted peacefully at the edge of the water playing with his pail and shovel.

Suddenly out of the gentle surf came a gigantic wave that immersed the little boy and, receding, swept him out into the cold Atlantic.

"Help! Help!" Hannah screamed, looking in vain for a lifeguard. "O dear God," she implored, "save him. I know I've never been religious. But please, God, save Sydney. Save him and I'll never ask you for anything again!"

The little boy disappeared in the booming surf, going under water for the third time. Hannah screamed again, beseeching God to save Sydney.

Heaven was attentive. Suddenly the sea threw the child back on the beach, where he lay coughing and crying. Hannah picked him up and pressed him to her breast and walked back up on the dry sand. She lay him carefully on her blanket and then turned to look up at the heavens.

"Listen, God, he had a hat, you know!"

■

The married daughter is crying into the telephone.

"Hello, Ma?"

"Darling, what's the matter? You don't sound so good."

"Oh, Ma, *everything's* the matter! Both kids got chicken pox. The refrigerator, full of food, broke down and I can't get a repairman. The sink's backed up and is running all over the kitchen floor. And in two hours my bridge club will be here for lunch. I'm going crazy! What am I going to do?"

"Darling, stop worrying. Your father's got the car but I'll take the bus to the station and the Long Island Railroad and a cab from the station. I'll clean up and take care of the kids and cook a nice lunch for you and the bridge club ladies. You got absolutely nothing to worry. I'll even make dinner for Lenny."

"Lenny? Who's Lenny?"

"*Lenny,* your husband."

"But Ma—oh, wait a minute—my husband is Harold. Is this 433-1854?"

"No, this is 433-1584."

(Long pause) "O my God! Does this mean you're not coming?"

A *nebbish* was trying to back his car into a parking space at the curb. A policeman walks over.

"Officer," the *nebbish* asks, "is it okay to park here?"

"Absolutely not! Fifth Avenue's restricted."

"Then how is it that all those other cars are already parked?"

The policeman sneered, "They didn't ask!"

■

Customer at the Broadway Delicatessen: "You're positive you're the waiter I gave my order to?"

Waiter: "Of course. What made you ask?"

Customer: "By this time I expected a much older man."

■

An elderly Canal Street Jewish storekeeper is knocked down by a taxi and brought to St. Vincent's Hospital. A crisply starched nursing nun gently tucks him into bed and asks, "Mr. Abelson, are you comfortable?"

He nods. "I make a nice living."

■

Ginsburg took his grandson to the Barnum & Bailey Circus at Madison Square Garden. A man with a violin bowed to the spectators and coolly slid himself into the mouth of a cannon, violin and bow in hand.

There was a terrific explosion, clouds of smoke, and the violinist was hurled high into the air. While still aloft, he managed to scratch out a few notes, before landing in the great net across the arena.

The crowd screamed and applauded. Eyes wide and popping, the little grandson said, excitedly, "Wow! Grandpa, wasn't that neat! What do you think?"

The old man shrugged. "Not bad. But a Heifetz he ain't."

■

Florence Noodleman took her small son to Brighton Beach. She spread out her blanket, put up their beach umbrella, and shook her finger at him.

"Sheldon, don't fool around in the sand, it'll get in your eyes.

And come out of the sun, you'll get heat prostration. Don't go in the water, it's over your head!"

She shook her head sadly, complaining to the heavens, "*Oy vay,* such a nervous child!"

■

Emma Trachtman, well past eighty, decides to make out her will. She goes to her rabbi to discuss the details and to have some religious questions answered. After her few wordly goods are finally allotted, she tells the rabbi that she wants to be cremated. He strongly protests, Judaism does not sanction cremation. But she sticks to her guns, nothing will change her mind.

"But why?" wheedles the rabbi.

"It's my ashes," the old woman says, as if that explained everything. "I want my ashes scattered over Bloomingdale's."

"*Bloomingdale's?*" the rabbi says. "I don't understand."

"That way I'll be sure my daughters will visit me twice a week."

Boris Thomashefsky, star of the Yiddish Theatre, boasted that the only time he slept alone was when he was sick—and that wasn't very often. Night after night women waited for him outside the stage door.

One night he took a luscious young thing to bed, and in the morning, as was his custom, he presented her with two orchestra tickets for that night's performance.

Obviously disappointed, the young thing burst into tears.

"My darling," rumbled the Great One, "whatever is the matter?"

"Oh, Mr. Thomashefsky," she sniffed, "I am poor. Tickets aren't what I need. I need bread!"

"Bread!" boomed Thomashefsky, "Bread! Thomashefsky gives tickets. You want bread? Go screw a baker!"

■

Goodman, a confirmed Manhattan dweller, after years of nagging by his wife, finally agreed to move to Westchester County. An old friend met him on the commuter train and asked him how he liked it.

Goodman shrugged. "At first I never thought I could stand it. But then I got a paramour and now everything's fine."

"*You*, you got a paramour? That's a disgrace at your age. What does your wife say?"

"My wife?" said Goodman. "Why the hell should she care how I cut the grass?"

■

Two Manhattan mothers met in Central Park. The first was carrying her groceries, the second pushing a tandem carriage with two baby boys in it.

"Good afternoon, Mrs. Klipstein. A pair of absolute angels you got there. Tell me something. How old are they?"

Mrs. Klipstein swelled with pride. "The lawyer is two and the doctor is three."

■

Friends and relatives filed past the open coffin, sniffling and sighing. Mrs. Tannenbaum said to a friend, "You'd think he was just sleeping. Look at him—tan, relaxed...so healthy."

"Why shouldn't he be?" replied her friend. "He just came back from two weeks in Miami."

■

Two old men were feeding the pigeons in front of the Museum of Natural History. "So, Moishe, how's everything going?" one asked.

"Lousy!" said the other. "Last month alone on doctors and medicines, I spent three hundred dollars!"

"In one month? Back in Russia you could have been sick a couple of *years* for that kind of money!"

■

The waiter at the Broadway Delicatessen watched in disbelief as his customer bent over the herring he had brought him and began talking to it.

"Hey, mister," the waiter asked, "what do you think you're doing?"

"I'm talking to the fish."

"You can talk to *fish?*"

"Certainly. I know seven different fish languages."

"Well, well—so what did you tell him?"

"I asked him where he came from and he answered from Great Neck Bay. I used to live near there so I asked him how's things in Great Neck? And he answered, 'How should I know? I ain't been there for years!'"

■

Two senior citizens were sunning themselves on a Central Park bench—not saying a word. Minutes ticked by. Finally one said, "So tell me, how are things going?"

The other made a face and shrugged. "How about yourself?"

"Mn-yeh."

They both stood up.

The first one said, "Well, so long. It's certainly nice to have a confidential talk."

■

At the Plaza, an *alrightnikeh* from Chicago said to her husband, "Melvin, did I have a dream last night! I dreamed you bought me a mink coat!"

He smiled and patted her shoulder. "In your next dream you should wear it in good health!"

■

Two West End Avenue apartment-house neighbors were talking. One said, "You heard the news? There's a rapist in the building!"

The other nodded. "I know, I gave already."

■

A man walked in to Moskowitz and Lupowitz's East Side restaurant and was surprised to see his waiter was Chinese. He was more surprised when he asked for London broil and the Oriental shook his head and whispered *"nisht gut"* (Yiddish for "not good").

When the man went to pay his bill at the cashier's counter, he asked the boss where he ever got a Chinese who could talk Yiddish.

The boss leaned toward him and whispered, "Shhh! He thinks I'm teaching him English."

■

One Seventh Avenue dress manufacturer was talking to another. "The damnedest thing happened. You remember Plotnick? Now he's fooling around with his models!"

His friend shrugged. "So what else is new? Everyone in the trade does it. I've even done it myself."

"Oh yeah?" his friend said. "But you forgot that Plotnick's now in *men's* clothing!"

■

Klutznick had absolutely no luck with horses. Day after day he picked losers at Aqueduct and Belmont. When his money was on them, favorites lost and long shots never came in. One day a friend who was just as successful at the track as he was unsuccessful, felt sorry for him and gave him a "sure thing."

"Put your money on Finagle in the fourth. At twenty to one you can't lose." Klutznick was thrilled. Right from the starting gate Finagle took the lead and kept increasing the distance between him and the pack. Then, suddenly, at the two-thirds mark, the horse ran off the track, dashed through the exit, and out of sight.

Klutznick screamed. "Luck like mine there never was in the whole history of the world. This is the first time a jockey suddenly decided to steal a horse!"

■

A suddenly successful New York Jewish TV writer, newly arrived in Hollywood, bought a small seagoing yacht and a fancy uniform to match. Eager to impress his old mother, he invited her for a sail. Standing proudly at the wheel, he pointed to his cap. "Look, Mama, now I'm a captain!"

She put her hand on his arm. "Sammeleh," she said, "by me you're a captain. By you you're a captain. But by captains, you ain't a captain!"

■

Finkelstein, the delicatessen owner, was being grilled by two men from the IRS. He said, "What are you giving me? I kill myself working twelve hours a day to make a living for my wife and family and you got the *chutzpa* to question my fifteen-thousand-dollar-a-year income?"

"No, Mr. Finkelstein," one of the men responded, "we're not questioning your income. We're questioning those four trips to Israel that you and your family made last year as a business expense."

"Oh, that," shrugged Finkelstein, "I forgot to mention that we also deliver."

■

"Mommy," asked the precocious five-year-old, as she saw two dogs copulating, "what are those doggies doing?"

"Darling," said her mother, "the little dog, underneath, is very sick, so the big dog is pushing him to Mt. Sinai Hospital."

■

Judge "Honest Abe" Feldman asked the attorneys for the plaintiff and the defense to approach the bench. He peered over his glasses. "I have here, from the defendant, a campaign contribution for my reelection for five thousand dollars." He paused. "And here, from the plaintiff, for the same purpose, a contribution of twenty-five hundred.

"Now, in order to judge this case purely on its merits, without fear of favor, absolutely fair and square, with no hanky-panky, I must ask the plaintiff to come up with another twenty-five hundred dollars."

■

At Rosemarie de Paris, the fanciest patisserie on Fifth Avenue, Mrs. Tannenbaum dropped in for some *nosherei*. After inspecting the luscious wares, she said to the supercilious blonde behind the counter, "Please, you should gimme two pounds of those chocolates."

The haughty one said, "Modom means the bonbons, no doubt?"

"Yeah. And also, please, three pounds of those fancy cookies."

"Ah," breathed Her Highness, "our petit fours. Shall we deliver these in our Rolls-Royce limousine waiting at the curb?"

"Nah, you shouldn't bother. I'll take them with me."

This was too much for the saleswoman. She drew herself up proudly. "Modom, from Rosemarie de Paris you don't *shlep!*"

■

At a Manhattan house party a guest was interrupted by his host when he began to tell a story. He had gotten as far as, "It seems that these two Jews, Levy and Rabinowitz..."

"Why does it always have to be two *Jews*? Couldn't it just as well be two Irishmen or two Greeks? Why are we always the funny people?"

"You're absolutely right," said the raconteur. "I'll start over. There were these two Chinamen, Wong Tah and Fu Sing and they're hustling to the synagogue for a Bar Mitzvah..."

■

A friend asked Lefkowitz how his new line of sportswear was going.

Lefkowitz groaned. "I'll show you." He walked his friend into the factory and flung open a door. Countless rows of separates filled the whole enormous loft. "Ten thousand, twelve thousand outfits I got hanging on those racks. You see any of them moving? You see any customers? You ask how things are going? They ain't."

"But it's a beautiful inventory," his friend said. "With those partners of yours, you'll move them. They're smart. What are they doing?"

"My partners," sneered the manufacturer, "my partners? *They're hanging in the closets!*"

■

In a shoe store in a poor section of Brooklyn, Nudelman was laying down the law to a new clerk. "Remember, here it's strictly cash and carry. No credit. Don't let a pair of shoes get out of the store without full payment."

A customer came in and the clerk sold him a pair of shoes. As the purchaser left he said, "I only got two dollars on me. I'll bring the rest of the money tomorrow."

Nudelman rushed over but he was too late, the man was gone. "What the hell kind of a stupid transaction was that?" he yelled. "That bum will never come back with the money. Didn't you hear what I told you?"

"About this you shouldn't worry," answered the clerk. "He'll be back. I gave him two left shoes."

■

At one time New York's Canal Street was lined with men's and boys' clothing stores. Customers from fifty miles around came for "bargains." To help them make up their minds they window-shopped. The proprietors lounged in the doorway as "puller-in-ers."

A young man once stopped to look at a certain suit in a window. Before he could resist he was inside.

The proprietor released him and said, "Aha, I can see you got

good taste, you picked the best suit in the house. To show you I
like to do business with a man with such good taste, I'm going to
make you a one-time, special proposition. I wouldn't ask $65 for
the suit. I wouldn't ask $55. I wouldn't even ask you $45. To you,
my friend, one flat price—$35."

The young man said, "I wouldn't give you $35 and I wouldn't
give you $25. My offer is $22.50 flat."

The merchant smiled. "Sold! That's the way I like to do
business—no chiseling."

■

Melnick, well along in years, decided it was time to buy himself a
coffin and went to see his fellow lodge member, Marcus the
mortician.

"For a fellow lodge member, I got for you a special value. My
best solid bronze number, with engraved sterling-silver handles
and genuine silk, not rayon, lining. For you only, special, just
two thousand dollars."

Melnick, a born comparative shopper, said he would think
about it and left. He was back an hour later with fire in his eyes.

"What do you think, I'm a jerk or something? Some friend
you are! A complete stranger, Kugelman, down the street, who
doesn't know me from a hole in the wall, offers me the same
casket, solid bronze, the same sterling engraved handles and the
genuine silk satin lining for only fifteen hundred dollars and no
bargaining!"

"Don't be a *shmo!*" yelled Marcus. "You buy your coffin from
Kugelman, go ahead. But I'll tell you right now, six months after
they bury you your behind will be sticking out through the
bottom!"

■

Epstein finally managed to tear himself away from Seventh
Avenue and take a vacation in the Bahamas. He decided to try
his skill at skin diving and rented all the latest, complete
paraphernalia. Cautiously he lowered himself over the side of
the boat to the ocean bottom, where he trudged along in his big
flippers. He was suddenly astonished to encounter his biggest

competitor thrashing about wildly in nothing but a pair of swim trunks—no mask, no tank, no flippers, no gauges—nothing!

"Jake," he burbled through his mask, "what are you doing down here without even a mouthpiece?"

"What the hell do you think I'm doing," Jake gurgled. "I'm DROWNING!"

■

Feeblewitz was a clumsy shoplifter and they nabbed him in Tiffany's. "Give me a break," he pleaded, "I'll pay for the watch, okay?" The softhearted manager agreed and handed him the bill. Feeblewitz turned pale. "*Oy vay!* This is a lot more than I planned to spend. Can't you show me something less expensive?"

■

A man went into a famous Madison Avenue custom tailor to buy a suit. A distinguished-looking individual in a wing collar, striped pants, and a cutaway proceeded to interview him. He asked the customer's name, address, occupation, pastimes, political affiliation, and his wife's maiden name.

"What's with all the questions?" the man asked. "I ain't joining your club. All I want is a suit."

"Ah, my friend," the salesman said, "before we sell you a suit here we make certain that it fits your personality and your position in life. We send to England for the proper wool for you. From France we import just the right lining. And from Scotland the precise horn buttons you should have. Then, regardless of the number of fittings you may need, five tailors fit you to perfection."

"Well, that's too bad," the customer said, "because I need this suit for my daughter's wedding the day after tomorrow."

"You haven't a thing to worry about," the salesman assured him. "You'll have it."

■

Moe and his partner, Jake, were about to plunge into the pool at the YMHA when Moe suddenly clapped his hand to his forehead.

"*Oy, gevalt!* I was so happy we were taking the afternoon off that I forgot to close the safe!"

Jake shrugged. "*Nu,* so what's the difference? We're both here, ain't we?"

■

Tanta Zelda, a very conservative middle-aged Jewish lady, after much coaxing, was finally persuaded by her sporty nephew to accompany him to the Jamaica racetrack. Much against her principles, but he was so insistent, she bet five dollars on the daily double. Marvelous to relate, she won! As she was scooping up her winnings at the pari-mutuel window, she looked over her thick glasses and shook a warning forefinger at the payoff clerk.

"Now, young man," she said sternly, "I hope this will be a lesson to you!"

■

"Mrs. Glantzman," asked the talk-show host, "if you found a package with a million dollars in it on the street, what would you do?"

"That all depends," the elegantly dressed visitor answered. "If I found it belonged to somebody very poor, I'd give it back."

■

Sam Levenson had a cat, Daisy, who was forever getting in his mother's way. Occasionally, in the dark, Mama Levenson would step on Daisy's paws. When the cat screeched she would always say in self-defense, "Who tells it to walk around barefoot?"

■

When Levenson was a Manhattan public-school teacher he once asked a fourth-grader, "Why did you hit Gabe?" The boy answered, "Because he hit me back first!"

■

Yeshiva student: "Dad, how come when I want a Coke you always tell me it will spoil my dinner, but a martini gives you an appetite?"

■

In a famous French restaurant, S.J. Perelman's wife asked him, "Dear, what are the snails like in here?"

S.J. said, "They're disguised as waiters."

■

The late owner of the Stage Door Delicatessen was a kind man who gave many a handout to the moochers who besieged him.

One night a particularly ragged one was promised a free meal just as soon as a large crowd of paying customers had been served.

This took longer than the hungry man thought it should. Finally he banged on his table and yelled at the owner, "Hey, I've been waiting nearly a half hour. How much longer do I have to wait?"

The perspiring owner looked at him over the top of his whirring slicing machine.

"What's the matter, you bum? You double-parked or something?"

■

Two visitors to New York were walking along the old Hudson River dock section when one pointed to a strange-looking freighter. "Hey, what kind of ship is that?" he asked.

His friend said, "It's Israeli."

"That's funny," the first answered, "it doesn't *look* Jewish."

■

"Do you realize," said a subway strap-hanger to a bearded citizen in a yarmulke seated before him reading the *Daily Forward,* "that you're reading your paper upside down?"

"Certainly I do," the old man snapped, "and don't think it's easy!"

■

Bloomberg was walking along Lower Broadway when a total stranger gave him a tremendous thump on the back and cried, "Hello, Pincus!"

"I'm not Pincus," said Bloomberg, "I don't even know anybody by that name."

"You're sure you're not?" the stranger asked. "Positive?"

"Of course I'm sure," Bloomberg said, "and even if I were, is that how to greet a friend, by punching him in the back?"

"Listen," said the stranger, "who the hell do you think you are to tell me how to greet Pincus?"

■

Two old Jewish men met at Fourteenth Street and Broadway as they stood waiting for the traffic light to change. The first said, "*Nu*, I been hearing some sad news about your family. My condolences. But tell me, who was it that died, you or your brother?"

■

Grossman and Epstein walked into Ratner's one afternoon for a pastry and a glass of tea. Grossman assumed a serious expression and beckoned the waiter. "But in a clean glass, please."

A few minutes later the waiter waddled back with the pastry and two glasses of tea. He peered through his thick lenses.

"Which one gets the clean glass?"

■

As always, Ratner's had its menu pasted on the window. The daily special was featured, "Meat, potato, and two green vegetables, $2.25." (This was a long time ago!)

Zuckerman went in and ordered it. The waiter set down boiled beef, potato, and string beans.

"Hey," Zuckerman yelled, waving the menu, "it says here *two* green vegetables. Where's the second green vegetable?"

"What's the matter," the waiter sneered, "the pickle is blue?"

■

The young woman reporter from the New York *Daily News* was assigned to do a human interest story for Father's Day. What better place for material than the Senior Citizens' Retirement Home? She arrived to find three particularly decrepit specimens seated together on a bench under a tree. She explained her assignment, had her photographer take their pictures, and explained that she would like each to give his particular recipe for longevity.

Said the first, "No secret to it, lady. Clean living's the answer. No whoring around, no alcohol, no tobacco, plenty of exercise, and sensible eating. I kept away from fats and sweets and watched my cholesterol. And look at me, I'm eighty-one and I could pass for seventy, easy!"

The reporter turned to the second. "How about you?"

He appeared in worse shape but spoke up briskly enough. "He's nuts! That abstinence business is for the birds. Moderation's the answer. Moderation in all things. I drank a little, couple of shots of schnapps to keep me going, smoked a couple of cigars a day, enjoyed cake and ice cream; good red meat and gravy; had a few girl friends from time to time. But in moderation, you understand. And look at me." He tottered to his feet and threw out his chest. You'd never know it but I'll be eighty-four on Passover."

The third old man blinked his watery eyes and cackled. "A pair of *shnooks*, both of them." He coughed, shaking his frame convulsively. Then with great effort he pulled himself erect, leaning on his cane. Pasty-faced, he gave his prescription for longevity:

"Life is for living! I lived. Three–four packs of Camels a day, a fifth of bourbon a day, and a couple glasses of beer when I was thirsty. Eat? Had an appetite like a horse. Ate everything and anything. Loved dairy especially, lots of sour cream and cottage cheese—ice cream, cheesecake, strudel. And chocolate, I loved candy. Couldn't let the girls sleep alone, either. Had only three wives but I must have slept with a hundred. God gave me the equipment and I used it. That's how I lived and why I'm still here today."

The reporter marveled. It certainly was a strange formula for a healthy old age! She paused in her note-taking. "Well, you certainly surprise me. Tell me, how old are you?"

He grinned, exposing his naked gums. "Fifty-four, the third of last month."

■

A young man, walking home past a cemetery, is distressed to see an old man sitting on the curb, beating his breast and weeping bitterly. He is sobbing, "Both of them, dear God, my two beautiful daughters. Laying there in the cemetery! *Oy vay iz mir!*"

The young man walked over to him, wanting to give comfort

but embarrassed. Not knowing what to do, he handed the old man a Kleenex and patted him on the shoulder.

"My two beautiful daughters laying there in the cemetery. Better they should be dead!"

■

Horowitz is sitting reading quietly in his living room on West End Avenue when a large rock smashes through the window. Wrapped around it is a piece of paper. He opens it and reads, "Dear Mr. Horowitz: Unless you deposit ten thousand dollars in small bills in a package, in the rubbish container at the end of your block by no later than noon tomorrow, we will kidnap your wife. Sincerely yours, your neighborhood kidnaper."

He studies the note and then goes to his desk. He writes: Dear Kidnaper: Your rock of the thirteenth instant on hand. Unfortunately I do not have ten thousand dollars. But please keep in touch, your proposition interests me."

■

In an uptown cemetery a man is moaning aloud, over and over, "Oh, why did you die? Oh, why did you die?" This goes on and on until a woman putting flowers on a nearby grave says to him, "Who was it who died, mister? A close member of your family?"

The man shook his head no, and started wailing again, "Oh, why did you have to die?"

The woman says, "A very dear friend then?"

The man says, "No, as a matter of fact I never met him."

"Then why is his death so painful? Who is lying in that grave?"

"My wife's first husband."

■

Two Seventh Avenue button salesmen were standing eating hot dogs out in front of their building. One says to the other, "Say, do me a favor, lend me twenty dollars, will ya?"

His friend fishes in his wallet, pulls out a ten-dollar bill, and hands it to him.

"What's the matter, I ask you for twenty dollars and you hand me ten?"

"So why are you complaining? This way it won't be a total loss. I'll lose ten and you'll lose ten.

■

A lining jobber asks his friend for a loan of fifty dollars. "Look, I'll give it back as soon as I get back from Chicago."

"*Nu*, so when's that? When are you coming back?

The other shrugged, pocketing the money. "So who's going?"

■

Larry and Moe had a smash season. Every garment in the line was a "clicker." *Women's Wear* gave them a write-up, all the creditors were nearly paid off, and they were heavy with cash. It was time for a celebration.

Larry said, "We'll go to La Maison and order the best in the place—price no object." Moe agreed.

But, unfortunately, in this grand establishment where they had never dared venture before, the entire menu was in French.

"What's to worry?" said Larry. "We want the best, we'll get the best. We simply pick the most expensive."

He called over the maître d' and pointed at something for a hundred dollars. "Gimme that," he said, "and the same for my partner!"

The man's eyebrows went up, but he nodded, said, *"Oui, monsieur,"* and departed. After a long wait, two waiters arrived carrying between them a huge tray covered by a silver dome. Before they could set it down on the serving table, two more waiters arrived with another tray.

With a flourish they removed the covers. On each tray was a nicely browned suckling pig with an apple in its mouth.

Larry and Moe's eyes bugged. Moe exploded, "We can't eat that—it's pork!"

Larry sneered. "Don't show your ignorance. That's the way they serve baked apple in here!"

■

A short, energetic Jew pushed and shoved his way into a crowded Fifth Avenue bus. He sees a friend seated in front of him. "I see you couldn't get a cab either."

■

A rough-looking character walked up to a tourist near the Plaza Hotel and asked, "Pardon me, but do you know where Central Park is?"

The tourist said, "No, sorry I don't."

"Okay then, so I'll have to mug you here."

■

A Jewish businessman was recommending his Manhattan lawyer to a worried friend. "I got a lawyer for you, so stop worrying. He kept me out of jail by having the charge of sodomy changed to walking...too close."

10

They Aren't Telling Many Jewish Jokes in Israel

In any collection of Jewish humor, most of which comes from Eastern Europe and the United States, it seemed only reasonable to include some jokes from Israel as well.

Strangely, none of my sizable circle of dedicated joke-tellers knew any. There were a few short, funny stories, using Israel as a background that, a few years ago, did find their way into the records and tapes of top comedians like Myron Cohen and Lou Jacoby. But they are all singularly dated, largely concerned with the Israel-Egypt wars—exaggerating the prowess of Israel's fighting force and depicting the Egyptians as sort of Keystone Kops.

From the few Israelis I know—friends and relatives—it appears that Israeli humor is very unfunny here, primarily because it is "insider" stuff—topical, political, and local. It is seldom about sex and very largely about war, money, politics, and politicians in a struggling new nation. Moreover, much of the humor is not in the least "Jewish" and reflects, rather, the diverse ethnic backgrounds of its immigrant population. What *is* Jewish, is derivative of the traditional Ashkenazic humor of the shtetl—already adequately covered elsewhere in this book.

I am reasonably diligent at research and when my joke-telling pals couldn't come up with any Israeli jokes, I tackled the usual sources: libraries (general and specialized), publishers, and booksellers. I wrote, phoned, and made personal calls.

The only truly funny stuff I encountered was the writing of Ephraim Kishon, acknowledgedly Israel's outstanding humorist and premier satirist. Budapest-born, he lives in Tel Aviv, writes in Hebrew, and has as his target the idiocies of Israel's fanatics, wedding customs, telephones, TV, radio, traffic, taxes, bureaucracy, politics, women's fashions, et al.

Kishon writes short stories, books, plays, and films, many of which are excruciatingly funny and highly recommended. Yes, they are available in English. But none of this is "jokes" and all too long for inclusion here.

Along the trail I asked the owner of a large, progressive bookstore to make inquiries at a national bookseller's convention. What Israeli joke books were there? Published here or there. She found nothing. Finally, one large book distributor who bragged that his mighty computer was supposed to have "over a million titles" in it, came up with *one* book of Israeli humor, which I ordered.

It never arrived. I felt this explanation for our limited Israeli selection was in order

■   ■   ■

A man was just about to jump into the Sea of Galilee when an Israeli policeman grabbed him. "No! Don't do it! How can a good Jew in the prime of life think of suicide?"

"Because I don't want to live anymore!"

"But if you jump I'll have to go in after you and I can't swim. I would drown. And I have a wife and two children. You don't want such a thing on your conscience. Be reasonable. Perform a real *mitzvah*. Go back home. And there, in the comfort of your own home, hang yourself."

■

A picture of an Israeli newspaper, during the Pope's celebrated visit in 1964, showed him with the president of Israel. The caption greatly helped the mystified readers: "The Pope is the one with the yarmulke."

■

Ben-Gurion offered to guide a recently deceased Israeli through both heaven and hell so that he could decide where to spend eternity. He went first to heaven, which was filled with pink clouds; angels with harps; heavenly choruses; and soft, perfumed breezes.

Then he went to look at hell. It was a marvelous place—with wonderful parties, wild gambling, beautiful women, sparkling wines, sumptuous food, and bargains in everything. Without hesitation the Israeli cried, "Send me to hell!"

A moment later he was shaking his head in horror. Demons with pitchforks appeared, there were seas of sulfur fire, people being tortured and flogged.

"Wait, wait!" the Israeli yelled at his departing guide. "What happened? You tricked me! The hell you showed me was so wonderful!"

"Not so," Ben-Gurion answered. "It just *looked* that way. The first time you saw it, you were only a tourist. But now you're a permanent resident."

■

Six Arabs were about to shoot two captured Israelis. One of the Israelis said to the other, "I think I'm going to ask to be blindfolded."

The other said, "Look, Sam, don't make trouble!"

■

The top reporter on Israel's leading daily, *Maariv*, made a scoop. He was right on the spot when a gunman shot down a visiting notable. He ran to his car, whipped out its phone, and yelled to his city editor, "Stop the presses! Hold the back page!"

■

A Texan, visiting Israel, stops at a farmhouse for a drink of water. "What do you do?" he asks the man who lives there.

"I raise a few chickens," answered the Israeli.

"Do you all, now," says the Texan. "I'm a farmer myself. How much land do you have?"

The Israeli answers, "Fifty meters out front. But in back I have close to a hundred meters of property. What about your place?"

The Texan smiles. "Well, on my spread I have breakfast and get into my car and I drive and drive and don't reach the end of my ranch till suppertime."

"That's a shame," replied the Israeli, "I once had a car like that."

■

On the border, on top of a hill, is an Israeli guard. On the other side is an Arab guard. All day long the Israeli keeps shouting, "Thirteen, thirteen, thirteen."

This annoys the Arab, who finally shouts at him, "Crazy Jew, why are you hollering 'thirteen' all day? There's nothing or nobody around here. Thirteen what?"

The Israeli says, "You really want to know? Come here and I'll show you. There, now look over the cliff."

He kicks the Arab over the cliff, clears his throat, and starts yelling, "Fourteen, fourteen, fourteen!"

■

Cohen and Frumpkin, wealthy dress manufacturers, were in Israel for the first time and had dropped into a Tel Aviv nightclub. A new comedian was going through his highly successful monologue in Hebrew.

Cohen roared with laughter at each joke; Frumpkin listened in absolute silence.

When the comedian finished to tumultuous applause, Frumpkin said, "You certainly enjoyed that guy's act. How come? I never knew you understood Hebrew."

"I don't, not a word of it," admitted Cohen.

"So how come you laughed so much at what he was saying?"

"Ah," smiled Cohen, "because I *trusted* him."

■

The whole world was terrified. Scientists everywhere agreed that a new flood was imminent. Nothing could be done to prevent it. The waters were going to wipe out the world.

On TV, the leader of Buddhism pleaded with everyone to become a Buddhist. By so doing they would at least find salvation in heaven. The Pope gave a similar message on a worldwide hookup: "It is still not too late to accept Jesus!"

The Chief Rabbi of Israel took a more pragmatic approach: "We have three days in which to learn how to live underwater."

Avrim, an Israeli private, tried to wangle a three-day pass from his captain. "Not a chance," his captain told him. "You want a pass? In this army you got to earn it. Go do something spectacular and I'll give you a pass."

Two days later Avrim astounded everyone by capturing a brand-new Arab tank, single-handed. He got his pass along with a lot of publicity. Then, just three weeks later, he captured another and got a second pass and a lot of publicity. When he bagged his third tank, he became a national hero and was promoted to captain.

Some time later, Private Moishe, his first cousin, asked for a three-day pass. "Earn it, like I did," Avrim snapped.

"I couldn't," admitted Moishe, "I don't have your courage."

Captain Avrim locked his office door, pulled down the shades, beckoned Moishe to come close, and began to whisper. "Listen, Moishe. It's not as hard as you think. Here's all you do. Take one of our tanks out of the compound some night and drive out into the desert. Pretty soon you'll meet some Arab tank driver who is also looking for a three-day pass."

■

Nothing could be more democratic than the Israeli army. A sign in a barracks says: Privates Will Kindly Refrain from Giving Advice to Officers.

11

Nit Ahin, Nit Aher

Jewish jokes cover so many subjects, and originate in so many different times and places, that it is practically impossible to put them all into neat categories—although we have tried to do so wherever possible. So up 'til now we have:

- Rabbi jokes and stories
- New York jokes and stories
- Jokes about Chelm
- *Schnorrer* jokes
- *Shadchen* jokes
- *Luftmensh* jokes
- Israeli jokes
- One-liners
- Midrash stories
- Yiddish curses

So much for the obvious classifications. But the jokes and stories keep pouring in—widely varied in theme and tone, and bearing little if any relation to each other, so that further classification is impossible—so many are in a class by themselves.

So we've provided a catchall: *Nit Ahin, Nit Aher* (Neither One Thing nor Another)—a deep repository that defies categorization. Even so, we like to think there is a unifying element—two, in fact: They all make us laugh and, basically, they're all Jewish.

The greatest blizzard in a hundred years slammed down on Coldfoot, Nevada, and continued for four days, completely burying the town and all the roads leading to it. Snow lay four feet deep on the highway and as much as twenty in the drifts and mountain passes.

The huge, roaring rotary plows strained twenty-four hours a day, but it still took the better part of a week just to clear the main roads and drop food from helicopters to isolated ranchers and mountaineers.

High on an impassable mountain trail, unreachable by helicopter, was Meyer Shapiro's tiny cabin, buried in a deep drift. A Red Cross emergency team was organized to try and reach Meyer before he starved or froze to death, if he hadn't already. No one had seen any smoke from his chimney in days.

Powerful tractor plows and teams of men with shovels bent to the task and hour after hour dug the torturous miles to his buried door. The crew yelled for Meyer to answer them. There wasn't a sound. Finally, they dug out the door, pounded on it, and called his name.

Suddenly they heard a feeble scratching and a faint voice asked, "Who is it?"

The men cheered. Thank God, he was alive!

The leader shouted, "It's the Red Cross!"

The door opened the tiniest crack and the snow fell away. "Don't bother," Meyer said. "I gave by the office already!"

■

A stranger joined the funeral procession of the wealthiest man in town. He began crying and beating his breast, louder than anyone else.

Someone asked, "Are you a relative?"

"No."

"Then why are you crying?"

"That's why."

■

The psychiatrist shook his head sadly at the distressed woman. "I'm afraid there's nothing more we can do to make your husband get rid of the delusion that he is a chicken. We have tried psychotherapy now for six months. I'm afraid we'll have to put him in an institution."

The woman burst into tears. She shook her head. "No, no, you can't do that!"

"Why not, they'll treat him very gently."

"You don't understand, doctor—we need the eggs!"

■

Blanche led a very posh life at the Fontainebleau with her companions. She continually bragged about her two very successful sons—a *big* criminal lawyer and a *big* surgeon. Money was running from their ears and nothing was too good for their mother. They never forgot her birthday. But this year, God bless them, they were so busy with their clients and operations, they couldn't get down for her birthday. Instead they were sending fabulous presents: a Jaguar and a Picasso.

A few days after her birthday her friends asked if she had received her presents.

"Only one I got. The other is on the way."

"Which did you get?" a friend asked.

She smiled sheepishly. "To tell you the truth, I don't know."

■

The Hellmans and the Strudnicks were the social leaders (and deadly competitors) in the Jewish social life of their town. Whatever Claire Hellman did to make the society page in the *Cedarhurst Star*, Yetta Strudnick surpassed, or tried to, in the next week's paper. One social event after another, money flowed like water, and the community waited eagerly for the next competitive event.

Sidney Hellman's Bar Mitzvah celebration was the high-water mark of all such extravaganzas and no one could imagine anything more elegant. How could Gordon Strudnick's festivities top it?

When the time came, there were three orchestras under revolving colored lights; uniformed carhops; an entire hallway of hot, cold, and lukewarm hors d'oeuvres; large-grained caviar

in profusion; vintage champagne flowing from spotlighted fountains; and a gigantic ice-block sculpture of swans and sheep.

But Mrs. Strudnick produced an incredible triumph, the pièce de résistance: Centered at the end of the entrance hallway under a purple spotlight was a life-size sculpture of Gordon done in glistening chopped liver.

To this she expertly guided Mrs. Hellman, who, while her eyes popped, pretended that such things were, after all, nothing new to her.

"Mmmmm," she said, "not bad at all. Who done it, Schlepperman?"

"Nah," sneered the triumphant Mrs. Strudnick. "Schlepperman? Schlepperman works only in halvah!"

■

A sweet-looking, patient Jewish matron was explaining, with some embarrassment, that her sex life was kaput because Izzy's equipment was rigid as a clam. "Tell me, doctor, is there anything that can be done about it?"

The doctor asked her to send Izzy in. He came in and was annoyed. "What is she complaining about. I'm older so I don't get excited so often. Still, I get my semiannual erections."

The doctor reported this to the wife over the phone.

She sighed. "I only wish it were like that. All he gets is his annual semierections."

■

A convincing case can be made that it is not alone the love of money that makes so many young Jewish men go in for medicine. As one doctor explained it, it's wonderful to be able to tell a woman to take her clothes off, look her over without fear of interruption, and then send a bill to her husband.

■

At the turn of the century, two Parisian Jews got into a violent argument and agreed to settle it with a duel. At daybreak the following day, one awaited the other, pistol at the ready. Time went by—a half hour, an hour, an hour and a half. The missing duelist failed to show. Suddenly a messenger appeared and handed an envelope to the waiting duelist.

"Listen, Moishe, if I happen to be late, don't wait for me. Just go ahead and shoot!"

■

In mid-Atlantic a terrific storm broke out which stood the steamer on its beam ends and threw all the passengers about. The vessel rolled from side to side, women and children screamed in terror, and men strapped their dear ones in life belts and grimly awaiting the worst. An hysterical Jewish man shrieked, "God in heaven, save the ship! Oh, God, the ship is sinking, the ship is being smashed to pieces!"

An annoyed passenger tapped him on the shoulder. "What are you making such an uproar about? What are you screaming for? Is it your ship?"

■

An old Jewish man was in a Catholic hospital for an operation. The nurse asked who would pay his bill. The old man sighed. "My sister is my only living relative, but she can't pay the bill because she is an old maid. She converted to Catholicism and became a nun."

The nurse said, "You don't understand. We nuns are not old maids—we are all married to Jesus Christ."

"Oh, that's all right then," said the old man. "In that case send the bill to my brother-in-law."

■   ■   ■

Although he was long gone to his rest, no book of Jewish humor would be complete without some reference to that master of malapropism, that "Czar of all the Rushes," the Hollywood mogul, Samuel Goldwyn. Here are a few of his effusions.

■

Goldwyn had heard of Dorothy Parker's acid witticisms and wanted her to come to Hollywood and write for him. One of his assistants objected. "You don't want her," he said, "she's too caustic."

"What the hell do I care how much she costs?" Goldwyn shouted. "Get her!"

■

A famous French film, *La Prisonnière,* had been a smash hit abroad and Goldwyn was eager to buy the film rights. One of his directors shook his head sadly.

"You can't film that play [that was *then!*]. It's all about a bunch of lesbians."

"So what?" said Goldwyn. "We'll make them Americans."

■

At a top-level film conference, Goldwyn was reported to have said, "I'm willing to admit that I may not always be right, but I'm never wrong!"

■

Once, in England, Goldwyn was negotiating with George Bernard Shaw for film rights to his plays. Shaw was not eager to have them made into films and was making impossibly tough terms. Finally Goldwyn tried to appeal to the creative artist rather than the businessman.

"Look, Shaw, think of the millions who have never had a chance to see your plays on the stage. Think of the millions who will now have the opportunity to get acquainted with your art."

"Ah, Mr. Goldwyn," said the pixieish Shaw, "that's the difference between us. You think of nothing but art, while I think of nothing but money."

■

At an important conference, Goldwyn's top staff was attempting to change his mind about a project he was against. After a long argument, he shrugged and said, "Gentlemen, the best I can give you is a definite maybe."

Next day he called his staff together again. "I've reconsidered my decision. Gentlemen, you may include me out."

■

Goldwyn prided himself on his efficiency. In order to please him, his secretary told him one day, "Our files are so jammed, Mr. Goldwyn, that I suggest we destroy all correspondence over six years old."

"You got something there," said Goldwyn. "Just be sure to make copies."

■   ■   ■

"The food at Carleton Manor was awful," complained Mrs. Herzog. "Every mouthful was like poison. And, worse yet, the portions were so small!"

■

Jake was in the mood for love-making, but Sadie was not. "Sadie darling," he said, "lift up your nightgown." Sadie did not answer. Jake tried again. "Hey, Sadie, be a good wife. Lift up your nightgown."

Still Sadie didn't answer. Furious at being rebuffed, Jake jumped out of bed and ran out of the bedroom. In response, Sadie locked the door.

For nearly an hour Jake paced up and down the house. Then he came back to the bedroom and found the door locked. "Sadie," he yelled through the door, "I'm sorry I got sore. Open the door."

Sadie didn't answer. Now Jake was in a fury. "Goddamn it, Sadie, if you don't open the door, so help me God, I'll break it down!"

"You'll break it down?" said Sadie. "Look at mine Tarzan! A nightgown he can't lift up and now he's breaking down the door!"

■

Mrs. Fleischman had plenty of advice for her son, Herschel, before he embarked for Vietnam. "Get plenty of rest and don't eat fattening food in the army. Try to take a nap every afternoon. And if you're shooting Commies don't stay out too late."

"Mama," Herschel interrupted, "what do you think I should do if a Commie happens to kill me?"

Mrs. Fleischman sniffed. "You shouldn't talk so foolish, Herschel. What have the Communists got against you?"

■

"Don't laugh," Mrs. Goodman said to her friend attending their first American Kennel Club show together, "that skinny little dog over there is worth ten thousand dollars!"

"Ten thousand dollars? How could a dog save that much money?"

■

Bernstein had obviously been in a fight. A front tooth was missing, his nose dripped blood, and his jacket was torn.

"Darling, what happened?" his wife asked as she helped him into a chair.

"It's that damned Irish janitor," Bernstein explained. "He catches me in the hall and brags that he has laid every woman in the building except one, imagine!"

Mrs. Bernstein paused, wringing out a cold washcloth at the sink. "Hmpf, I bet it's that stuck-up Mrs. Weiss on the fourth floor!"

■

Bennett Cerf used to tell the story about the poor little Jewish tailor who slaved twelve hours a day in his grimy little shop to barely make ends meet. He had only one small indulgence. Every week he somehow scraped up a dollar to buy a lottery ticket. And for fourteen long years he never won a cent.

Then, late one day, two beautifully dressed young men stepped out of a stretch limo, slapped him on the back, and told him that he had won four million dollars.

His eyes streaming, the tailor yelled, "Ai-yi-yi!" locked up his shop, and threw the key down the sewer.

He bought himself suits Ronald Reagan would have envied, took a suite at the Plaza, and broke as many Commandments as he could. Soon he was supporting three models, a TV anchor woman, and an expensive crack habit. He drank and gambled, bought the Holland Tunnel and the Triborough Bridge, and caught three social diseases.

In one year he squandered the whole four mil and still owed the IRS.

Sick, exhausted, and disillusioned, he reopened his little

tailor shop and resumed his old ways. Habit was strong, however, and once again, each week he bought a lottery ticket.

Two years dragged by. And then, despite all theories to the contrary, lightning struck again. Another stretch limo appeared, and the two smiling passengers told him he had won first prize again!

The bent-over little tailor struggled to his feet from his position at the sewing machine.

"Oh my GOD!" he cried. "Do I have to go through all that again?"

■

A recent refugee was trying to sell an anti-Semite a bill of goods. The prospect explained that he bought only from Americans.

But the merchandise was so tempting and the refugee's protests of his loyal Americanism so strong that the anti-Semite bought several hundred dollars' worth of goods. As the refugee was repacking his sample case, he looked up and saw on the patriot's wall portraits of Washington and Lincoln.

"Nice-lookin' fellers," he commented. "Your partners?"

■

A customer of Fineman's Fish Store marveled at Fineman's quick wit and the fact that he had an answer for everything.

"Tell me, Fineman, we've been friends a long time, what makes you so smart?"

Fineman looked serious. "Look, I wouldn't tell everybody, but you I'll tell. It's herring heads. Eat enough of them and you could be positively brilliant."

"You got that kind here?"

"Sure, and they're only fifty cents apiece."

The customer took three. A week later he complained that he hadn't gotten any smarter.

"You didn't eat enough yet," Fineman said.

So this time the customer blew ten dollars for twenty fish heads. Two weeks later he was very angry. "Hey, Fineman, you're gypping me. You sell me a whole herring for fifteen cents. Why, should I pay you half a buck for a head?"

"You see," explained Fineman, "how much smarter you are already?"

■

In its window Grossman's antique gallery featured an ancient bed that "both George Washington and Napoleon slept in." Ida Farfinkle didn't believe it and challenged Grossman.

"How in the world could those two men have slept in one bed?"

"No trouble at all," said Grossman. "It's a double bed."

■

In Shanghai for the first time, Malkinson and Frumpkin slipped their guide some extra cash to be taken to a real opium den. There, with much grinning at each other, they both took a few puffs.

An hour later Malkinson boasted to his partner, "The stuff had no effect on me whatsoever."

"Me neither," said Frumpkin.

A few minutes later he thrust out his jaw. "I've made up my mind. I will buy control of IBM."

"The hell you will," Malkinson said. "I'm not selling."

■

Lawyer Silver was aghast when he walked into his apartment and found his wife, Nancy, walking on the ceiling.

"Hi," she said calmly.

"Hi? What do you mean, 'hi'? What are you doing walking on the ceiling? Don't you know it's against the law of gravity?"

There was a frightful crash as Nancy fell to the floor. Tenderly rubbing her bruised face she looked at him in a rage. "You had to open your big mouth, didn't you!"

■

Overheard in Moskowitz & Lupowitz's famous eatery: "Hey, waiter, this sauerkraut ain't sour enough!"

The waiter said, "You should pardon my mentioning it, but it ain't sauerkraut, it's noodles."

"Oh, okay. For noodles it's sour enough."

■

The snobbish young man from Virginia sniffed at Cohen. "I'll have you know that I'm from one of the First Families of Virginia. As a matter of fact one of my ancestors signed the Declaration of Independence."

Cohen yawned. "Big deal! One of my ancestors signed the Ten Commandments."

■

Mrs. H. Wellington Pincus gave an afternoon tea to welcome the new rabbi. "Please," she urged him, "Have another piece of strudel."

The rabbi held up his hand in protest. "Thank you, dear lady, but I've already had two."

"You've had four," corrected Mrs. Pincus, "but who's counting?"

■

Sam sat broiling in the sun in his rented rowboat, supposed to be enjoying his expensive fishing vacation. Hour after hour he tried. But the fish weren't biting. He tried worms, frogs, four kinds of artificial bait. No luck. Finally, utterly disgusted, he reeled in his line, dug into his pocket, and threw a handful of coins into the lake.

"*Nu,*" he hollered, "you don't like what I got, go buy yourself something you *do* like!"

■

For the fifth time Goldstein teed up his ball and swung with all his might. He watched with joy as a small object flew away at a sharp angle. "Aha!" he exulted to his caddy. "That time I got the ball away fine!"

The caddy sighed. "Mister, the ball is right where you put it. That was your wristwatch!"

■

Seated on the porch of Rosenthal's Rest in the Catskills are two *zaftig* matrons trying to impress each other with the importance of their husbands' positions.

"My Louie," said the first, "holds a very responsible position. Whatever goes wrong in that whole big factory, he's responsible."

■

A penniless Jewish boy of eleven, Abramowitz, immigrated to America in the steerage in 1920 and worked his way westward from New York. Now, sixty years later, he was a millionaire, living luxuriously at Aspen in the Rockies.

At a testimonial dinner in his honor, he exulted, "Only in America could this happen. Sixty years ago I didn't have a dime. And today I'm senior partner of Fidelman and O'Rourke. And, this is the most wonderful part: *I'm* O'Rourke!"

■

At a very elegant hotel in the Caribbean, Goldstein was trying to hasten his wife's dressing. "Should I wear my Mainbocher dress or the Christian Dior?" she asked.

"Wear the Dior," he said.

"And my furs? Should it be the chinchilla or the sable?"

"The sable," he said.

"And the perfume?" Should I put on the Arpège or the Joy?"

He exploded. "I don't give a goddamn if you smear on chicken *shmaltz!* But for God's sake come on downstairs for breakfast!"

■

Abe shocked his sixty-year-old son by announcing that he had just married a fifty-year-old woman.

"Married?" yelped his son. "Pa, are you crazy? You were just eighty-seven. What the devil did you get married for?"

"For companionship, what then?" countered the old man. "If you don't think it's lonely living all by yourself with no one to talk to, you don't understand. Now I got love and affection and a young wife to take care of me."

"Love and affection," mocked his son. "What love and affection? Without sex that's just talk. And you're too old for sex."

"Who's too old?" challenged his father. "We got plenty of sex almost every night!"

"Almost every night!" his son exclaimed.

"Yeah, almost every night. Almost on Monday, almost on Tuesday, almost on Wednesday, almost..."

■

Pincus beckoned to his waiter. *"Boychik,* this soup is cold," he said without even tasting it. "Soup I want hot."

The waiter brought in another plateful. Without so much as lifting a spoon, Pincus said, "It's not hot enough! I want it hot."

The exasperated waiter brought in a third plate of soup. Pincus sat with his arms folded and shook his head. "Also not hot enough!"

The waiter, now furious, said, "*Nu,* so how do you know this? You ain't even tasted it!"

"Positive," said Pincus. "So long as you can keep your thumb in it, it ain't hot enough!"

■

"Hey, *shmendrick,*" said Shlepperman, "you're always talking about relativity, Einstein's theory of relativity. What the hell is it? Can you maybe explain?"

"Sure, it's like this. You go to the dentist to have a tooth pulled. You are in the chair, maybe twenty minutes, actually. But it hurts so much you feel like you've been there an hour. On the other hand, you go to see a good Broadway show. Three hours you're sitting in the theater enjoying yourself. It's so good the time flies. When it's over it feels like only five minutes. That's relativity."

Shlepperman nodded dubiously. "I see," he said. "But tell me something. From this, Einstein made a living?"

■

An old Jewish woman was very curious about the nudist colony near her house and peered through a knothole in the fence around it. Suddenly she recoiled.

"Feh!" she exclaimed, "*Alla goyim!* [They're all Christians]"

■

Mrs. Ginsberg's good friend rushed in and told her that Mr. Ginsberg was chasing after a young chick. Mrs. Ginsberg shrugged. "*Nu,* so what?"

"This doesn't bother you?" her friend asked.

Mrs. Ginsberg smiled. "Why should it bother me? I got a little dog that chases cars, too."

An old woman was asked how you said, in Yiddish, "I'm sorry. I didn't hear you. Would you mind repeating what you just said?"

The old woman answered, *"Hah?"*

■

Lapidus, the animal lover, bragged to his friend, "It's a miracle, this strange power I got over dumb animals. Cats, dogs, sheep, horses. They all come up and lick my hand."

"Hah," said his friend, "some miracle! If you ate with a knife and fork once in a while they wouldn't be so friendly."

■ ■ ■

This next joke exists in at least three versions and was once used as the basis for an elaborate Lou Jacoby record routine. They all have the identical point and punch line—although one places the action in Nazi Germany, one in Israel, and one in New York, which is our version.

■

A Broadway casting director sent out a call for a Texan, over six feet tall, weighing well over two hundred pounds. Just at closing time, at the end of a particularly exasperating day, he gets a phone call from a man with a thick Jewish accent.

"Sorry," the casting director says, "you don't sound like a Texan to me."

"I'm not. I'm from the Bronx."

The director says, "Well, maybe we can get around that. But are you at least six feet tall and over two hundred pounds?"

"No, I'm exactly five-five and weigh one hundred and twelve."

Furious, the director yells, "Then what the hell are you calling me for?"

The voice replied, "Just to let you know that on me you shouldn't depend!"

■ ■ ■

After a hiatus of many years, interest in the tunnel under the English Channel was revived and several world-renowned engineering firms bid on the gigantic project. Their bids were all in the area of a hundred million pounds. And then an entirely unheard-of outfit, Herzog & Herzog, estimated that they could do the job for half as much. Much amused, the commissioner in charge of receiving bids sent for the Herzogs. He said, "I don't think you quite realize what's involved here. Your estimate is incredible. How in the world do you figure you can do this tremendous job for only fifty million pounds?"

"Nothing to it," said the first Herzog. "My brother takes a shovel and begins digging from the French side. I take a shovel and begin digging from England. We meet in the middle and that's all there is to it."

The commissioner was astounded. "Do you realize that the tiniest error in calculation will mean that you completely miss each other under the middle of the English Channel?"

Herzog shrugged. "All part of the game. So what? If that happens you'll come out way ahead. Instead of one tunnel you'll have two!"

■

Morganstern was very rich and very horny, too. His new, fresh-faced secretary with the high, full bosom, nice rounded tush, and long sexy legs really turned him on. He turned her on, too, and it wasn't very long before they wound up in the sack.

They enjoyed lunch hour "matinees," evenings of dalliance, and many country weekends. As often follows such pleasures, she found herself pregnant and tearfully confessed all to her mother.

The old warrior was furious that this rich, powerful man had taken advantage of her innocent daughter, whose only reaction was a flood of tears. Her mother patted her. "That *momzer*, that *no-goodnik*, that bastard! You rest, darling, I'll handle him."

With fire in her eyes Mama confronted Morganstern. "You'll marry Naomi!" she screamed, waggling her forefinger under his nose.

He sighed. He was not entirely surprised. "No," he said. "That's impossible. I'm married already, with two fine boys. But though you might find this hard to believe, I really care for

Naomi and want to take care of her. A big lawsuit we don't need. It would hurt Naomi's reputation as well as mine. I'll take care of her."

"No abortions!" yelled Mama. "In this we don't believe. She's going to have the baby."

"Okay," said Morganstern, "fair enough. Like I told you, I'm sorry. So here's what I'll do. I'll deposit twenty-five thousand dollars in the bank in Naomi's name so she can take care of the child."

Mama sneered. "Twenty-five thousand? What's twenty-five thousand today? Today it's thirty-five, forty, with inflation."

"Okay," he said wearily. "Thirty-five, and I'll rent a nice apartment for her. Better yet. I'll buy a condo and let her use it rent free. There, is that fair enough?"

The mother nodded. "Yeah, yeah, fair enough, I guess." Then a horrible thought suddenly struck her. "But what, God forbid, if she miscarries and doesn't have the baby?"

He shrugged. "I certainly don't wish it on her. But under those circumstances, all bets are off."

The mother's face froze. "You mean you wouldn't give her a second chance?"

■

It was during the Battle of the Bulge. The exhausted platoon was cut off from their company, out of ammunition, and facing a wall of well-entrenched Germans, also out of ammunition. Orders were to overrun them. A tough, battle-worn sergeant faced his men.

"All right, you guys. This is it. We're going to charge those Nazis. It'll be man to man, cold steel. So fix your bayonets."

A little Jewish private spoke up. "Man to man? So please, sarge, show me my man. Maybe I can come to an understanding with him."

■

Otto H. Kahn, the late great Jewish financier, when driving through Manhattan's lower East Side, saw a small men's clothing store with a tremendous sign:

MOISHE KAHN
COUSIN OF OTTO H. KAHN

In a fury, Kahn instructed his attorneys to threaten suit if the man (who was absolutely no relative) did not remove the sign immediately. A week later he drove by to see if it had been removed. It had. In its place was an even larger sign:

MOISHE KAHN
FORMERLY COUSIN OF
OTTO KAHN

■

Two *zaftig* Mamas meet in the Fontainebleau bar. One says, "What did you do to your hair? It looks awful, almost like a wig."

The other says, "It is a wig."

The other Mama says, "You know, you could never tell."

■

A ten-year-old boy asked his storekeeper father, "Pop, what's ethics?"

His father said, "It's like this. A woman comes into the store and buys eight dollars worth of delicatessen. She pays me with a ten-dollar bill. But when I go to the cash register to make change, I see it's *two* ten-dollar bills stuck together. Now comes the question of ethics. Should I tell my partner?"

A panhandler came up to Shapiro. "Mister," he said, "I haven't tasted food for a week."

The kindhearted Shapiro patted him on the shoulder. "Don't worry. It still tastes the same."

■

Three scientists, suffering from radiation sickness, were given six months to live and told they could have anything they wanted. The first scientist, a Frenchman, opted for a villa on the Riviera and a beautiful woman. The second, an Englishman, wanted to have tea with the queen. The third scientist was a Jew. He wanted the opinion of another doctor.

■

Levine complained to the developer that his new house had grass growing through cracks in the living-room floor. The developer sniffed. "For what you paid, what do you expect, broccoli?"

■

A man walked into his doctor's office and complained, "Doc, I'm having sex only once a week."

"How old are you?" the doctor asked.

"Seventy-eight."

"You're seventy-eight and still having sex once a week? That's wonderful. What are you complaining about?"

"My friend, Izzy, is seventy-eight also. And he says he has sex six times a week."

The doctor patted him on the back. "So you tell him the same thing!"

■

A religious man had a dream that God commanded him to make himself younger. So he went to a gym and reduced; had a hair transplant; got a nose job, new teeth, and contact lenses. Next he went to Florida for a good tan.

Then, in all his fresh new good looks, he stepped off a curb and an eighteen-wheeler promptly sent him to heaven. To his fury, God didn't pay him the least attention.

He yelled at God, "Hey, it's me. You told me to make myself young and I did. It cost a fortune and now you don't even speak to me!"

God looked at him closely. "Don't holler at me, Irving. I simply didn't recognize you."

■

Lefkowitz said nothing when he found a dollar too much in his pay envelope. But the next week the pay clerk discovered his error and deducted a dollar from Lefkowitz's pay.

Lefkowitz squawked. The clerk said, "Funny you didn't complain last week when I gave you a dollar too much."

Lefkowitz nodded. "You're right. A guy can overlook one mistake, but when it happens twice it's time to complain."

■

First long-suffering B'nai B'rith member: "My wife is driving me crazy. Night after night she keeps dreaming that she's married to a millionaire!"

Second member: "I should be so lucky. You got nothing to complain. My wife keeps dreaming she's married to a millionaire, too—but in the daytime!"

■

Sarah and Max were enjoying their first visit to Hawaii, toasting on the sands of Waikiki. "Tell me something," Sarah said, "how do you pronounce the name of this place? Is it Hawaii or Havaii?"

Max said, "You got me. But that big brown-skinned native over there will know. I'll ask him."

He did. The big man smiled. "Havaii," he said.

Max said, "Thanks, mister."

The native said, "You're velcome."

■

Two New York dress manufacturers met at the pool of the Fontainebleau. "How's business?" the first asked. His friend made a face, "*Mnyeh!*"

The other man said, "Say, for this time of year that's pretty good!"

■

Two women delegates from Hadassah met at a convention in Las Vegas. They grabbed and kissed each other.

Irma said, "Shoil, doll, you look like a new woman! What have you been doing to yourself?"

Shirley said, "Promise me you won't tell anybody, I'll tell you a secret: I'm having an affair!"

"Really? When? And who's catering?"

Sadly, Heimowitz walked into the offices of the local funeral parlor. "I'm here to make arrangements for my wife's funeral."

The funeral director was astounded. "Your *wife*, Mr. Heimowitz? We buried her from here last year."

Heimowitz sighed. "That was my first wife, Rose. I'm talking to you about my second wife."

"Your *second*? I didn't know you had remarried. *Mazel tov!*"

■

"If I were Rockefeller," sighed the *melamed* (Hebrew teacher), "I'd be *richer* than Rockefeller."

His friend asked, "What do you mean? How could you be richer?"

"I would do a little teaching on the side."

■

A pair of *shlimazls*, deep in their wine, were philosophizing. Said the first, "When you consider how much heartbreak life has in it for us Jews, death is not really a misfortune. Many times I think it's better if a man is never born at all!"

"You're absolutely right," sighed the other. "But how many of us are that lucky? Not one in ten thousand!"

■

The little newsboy who stood on the corner in front of the bank had sold his last paper when a friend approached. "Hey, Hymie, how's about lending me five bucks 'til Tuesday?"

"Sorry, but I can't."

"What do you mean, you can't?"

"I made an agreement with the bank. They agreed not to sell newspapers if I promised never to lend money."

■

Korngold was bragging to his friends about his wonderful trip to Rome. "It was very nice. In fact we even had an audience with the Pope."

An impressed friend said, "With the Pope yet! So tell me, how did you like him?"

"He was very nice, a fine *mensch*. But *her* I didn't care for."

Goldstein was furious. For three months his tailor had been dragging out making a simple pair of gabardine pants. "What the hell you been doing in all that time? You know God made the whole universe in only six days."

"*Nu*," sighed the tailor, "so look at it!"

■

Mrs. Noodleman and Mrs. Kirscheimer were watching the young people around the pool. A young man walked out on the diving board.

"*Ai-yi-yi*," exclaimed Mrs. Kirscheimer, "did you ever see a pimpled *punim* like that? And such a nose, not only big but crooked. Little, mean eyes and a mouth like blubber. A potbelly too, he's got, like an old man."

Mrs. Noodleman sat up stiffly in her beach chair. Her voice was like ice. "I want you to know that's my son you're talking about!"

"Well," said Mrs. Kirscheimer, "you should know that on him it's becoming."

■

At her concerned daughter's insistence, Mrs. Epstein, seventy-five, went to a gynecologist for the first time. He took her medical history and then said, "All right, now please take off all your clothes."

Her face reddened and her old eyes popped.

"*Everything?*" she asked.

"Yes, everything.'

Her ancient jaw thrust forward and she waggled her finger under his now. "Tell me something, doctor. Does your mother know how you make a living?"

■

Panting and perspiring, a small, plump Jewish salesman with a heavy suitcase ran up to the American Airlines gate only to have it slammed shut in his face.

Hopelessly, he yelled through the slats, "Stop! Hold it! Wait for me!"

An old man sitting reading his Yiddish paper looked up at the disturbance.

"I missed the damned plane by thirty seconds," the salesman exploded. "Thirty lousy seconds!"

The old man grunted. "From all the *tummel* you're making, a person would think you had missed it by an hour!"

■

Groucho Marx wanted to join a very exclusive beach club at Newport Beach. A friend told him to forget it, the club was notoriously anti-Semitic.

"So what?" Groucho quipped. "My wife's a *shiksa*. Maybe they'll let my son go into the pool up to his knees."

■

Kornblum, an amateur mountain climber, decided one day that at last he had sufficient skill to scale Mount Horeb. As he inched his way upward, the crumbling rock broke off under his boot and Kornblum fell nearly two hundred feet, miraculously stopping his fall by grabbing the protruding branch of a small tree.

"Help! Help!" he yelled, swaying perilously.

Suddenly a great booming voice from above thundered, "My son, do you have faith in me?"

"Yes, yes, God, I do. I always have!"

"Do you now trust me implicitly?"

"Oh, God, yes!"

"Then let go of that branch."

"Let go?"

"I, the Lord thy God, tell you to release the branch."

There was a long pause as Kornblum hung there, sweating. Then he said, "Pardon me, but is there anyone else up there?"

■

Six-year-old Sammy got off the bus after his first day at school. His mother ran to meet him.

"So, darling, tell me, what did you learn?"

"I learned how to write, Mama!"

"Already, on the first day? A genius I got. So what did you write?"

"I don't know, Mama. I can't read yet."

∎

A woman stormed into Gottlieb's Laundry. "A first-class laundry you call yourselves? You do A-Number-One work? Ha! Take a look here what you did!"

Gottlieb studied the fabric in her hand. "Lady, I don't see anything wrong with this lace."

"Lace, you *momzer!* When I brought it in, it was a sheet!"

∎

Mrs. Plotnick looked down at her friend in the maternity ward. "So it's really true, you had triplets?"

"Absolutely. And according to the doctor, it only happens once in three million times!"

Mrs. Plotnick's eyes widened. "My God, Hannah, when did you find time to take care of the house?"

∎

Dr. Friedman was very successful. If his patients couldn't afford the operation, he touched up their X rays for them.

∎

When a jockey continued to hit his horse, the horse suddenly turned around and said, "Why do you keep hitting me? There's nobody behind us."

∎

Sol was sleeping soundly when his wife shook him awake. "*Oy,* Sol, I'm freezing. Go close the window. It's cold outside."

Groaning, he got out from under the covers, closed the window, and got back into bed. "*Nu,* Mrs. Fixit, so now it's warm outside?"

∎

A pretty young *tsatskeleh* asked the fur salesman if the rain would damage the new mink she was dickering for.

He sniffed. "What's to worry? You ever see a mink carry an umbrella?"

■

The smart young accountant sat sighing and praying in the synagogue. "O Master of the Universe, blessed be Thy name, if Thou wouldst grant me twenty-five thousand dollars, I promise to give twenty-five hundred to the poor. And, O Holy One, if Thou dost not trust me, or sees deceit in my heart, just deduct the twenty-five hundred in advance and simply give me the balance."

■

After five fittings and six alterations, Fineberg's expensive custom-tailored suit still fit like an unmade bed. "Suck in your stomach," the tailor said. "Now bend your left elbow and raise up your right shoulder. Now pull your hands back into your sleeves a little. See, now it fits like the paper on the wall. The cuffs are supposed to go over your shoes like that."

Disgusted, and trying to follow these instructions, Fineberg grabbed his hat and twisted out of the store.

A stranger tapped him on the shoulder. "I beg your pardon, but would you mind telling me who your tailor is?"

"That *shlemiel?*" Feinberg exploded. "Are you crazy? Why would anyone want him?"

"Because any tailor who can fit a cripple like you must be a genius!"

■

A pair of Martians who had arrived on different spaceships, ran into each other on Fifth Avenue.

The first asked, "So tell me, what's your name?"

"Five-two-six-seven-nine-three."

The first one squinted at him with his three eyes. "That's funny. You don't look Jewish!"

There was an old man who loved birds. His son, on a trip to South America, saw a magnificent toucan for sale. He thought, My father will go absolutely crazy over him.

So he bought the bird, which was terribly expensive, and arranged for the pet shop to ship it to his father, making absolutely certain that it would be adequately caged, watered, and fed.

His father met him at the airport when he returned and embraced him.

"Hey, Pop, how'd you like that toucan?" the son asked.

"Wonderful," said his father, "It was absolutely delicious!"

■

The doctor finished a thorough examination of an eighty-seven-year-old woman. He said, "Even modern medicine can't cure some things. There's nothing I can do that will make you any younger."

"Who asked for younger?" she snapped. "I want you to be sure I get older!"

■

"A dollar-fifty a pound for liver?" protested Mrs. Grobnick. "By Ginsberg is only a dollar twenty-five!"

"So go buy by Ginsberg," the butcher said.

"I certainly would, but just today he happens to be all out."

"He's robbing you," the butcher said. "When I'm out of liver I charge only a dollar fifteen."

■

A row of homes was destroyed by a fire. The community insurance adjuster was writing out checks to the victims. A man whose home was not involved got on the line for a share of the handout.

"Hey, mister, you don't belong on this line," the adjuster said. "You didn't suffer from the fire!"

"Suffer? You have no idea. I was scared to death!"

■

Goldblum didn't want to go in for a checkup, but he looked so terrible that his wife insisted. The doctor gave him a thorough going-over and shook his head.

"You're in bad shape, my friend. Tell me, do you drink?"

"Of course," said Goldblum. "I start every day with a bottle of vodka."

"And the way you cough, you must be a heavy smoker."

"Ever since I was fourteen I smoke a couple packs a day."

"Look, Goldblum, unless you change your ways you're not going to be around very long. You have to quit drinking and smoking immediately. And that's an order. No more, starting right now. And before you go you owe me forty dollars for my advice."

Goldblum stood up. "Who's taking it?"

■

The rich man of the family died and the heirs were all assembled for the reading of the will. The lawyer read: "To my wife, Lilly, I leave half of everything I own. To my son, Paul, I leave a third of the remainder. To my daughter, Shirley, the same. To my son, Melvin, the same. And to my brother-in-law, whom I promised to mention in my will—Hello, there, Sherman!"

■

Malkowitz, a New York hosiery salesman, found himself stranded in a rural Arkansas town that apparently had no restaurant. Tired and hungry, he parked in front of the general store on Main Street and walked in.

"You maybe handle fertilizer?" he asked.

"You bet," the man replied.

"That's fine. So go wash your hands and make me a nice cheese sandwich."

■

"Ah," said the first elderly member of the congregation to his neighbor, at the end of the service, "that cantor is absolutely magnificent!"

"What's the big deal," his friend answered. "If I had his voice, I'd sing just as well."

"This is my wife's birthday," the man explained to the clerk, "and I'd like to buy her a really beautiful bedside clock."

The clerk said, "A little surprise, eh?"

"Right," the man said, "she's expecting a Cadillac."

■

"Why did my wife divorce me?" a man said to his friend. "Purely for religious reasons. She worshiped money and I didn't have any."

■

A woman on flight 139 out of Las Vegas noticed an immense diamond on the finger of the enameled blonde next to her. It was truly eye-popping. Before she could avert her gaze, the woman saw her interest, smiled, and extended her hand so that the other woman could examine it more closely.

"Wow!" breathed the observer, "that's the biggest diamond I ever saw. It's magnificent. I'm sure it's famous."

"It is," said the owner. "A lot has been written about it. It's the Klipstein diamond. But a awful curse goes with it."

"A curse? What's the curse?"

"Klipstein!" she whispered.

■

A New York ribbon salesman was desperately trying to sell his goods in Georgia. But wherever he went he encountered sneering anti-Semitism.

Finally, in a big Atlanta department store the buyer mocked him. "All right, Izzy, I'll buy some of your ribbon. Just as much as reaches from the top of your Jewish nose to the tip of your Jewish prick!"

A week later the buyer was astounded to receive six hundred gross of top-quality ribbon. A note was enclosed with the invoice. "Thank you for your valued order, billed in accordance with your instructions. (signed) Isidore Marmelstein, residing in New York, circumcised in Vilna, USSR."

■

The *no-goodnik* was doing his best to unbutton the blouse of the pretty girl he had lured up to his room for a drink. But with all his soft talk she refused to let him get any further.

"Come on," he coaxed, "give me just one good reason why you won't."

"I'd hate myself in the morning!"

"Oh, is that all? So sleep late."

■

For years old man Briskin's friends had been begging him to get a hearing aid. One day he passed a store window that said:

GOING OUT OF BUSINESS
Everything must go: Radios, TVs, Hearing Aids
50% to 75% OFF!

Briskin went inside. Fifteen minutes later he was back outside with a hearing aid that had been reduced to only ten dollars. Just then his friend, Pearlman, came by and greeted him.

"Pearlman, look at this!" He pointed to his ear. "I finally bought a hearing aid. You were absolutely right. What a difference. Now I can hear like a ten-year-old."

"That's wonderful," said Pearlman. "What kind is it?"

Briskin looked at his wristwatch. "Half past four."

■

Old man Tannenbaum lowered himself into a chair in Futnick's barbershop. Futnick wrapped the cover around him and asked, "*Nu*, a haircut?"

"No," answered Tannenbaum, who had been waiting forty minutes, "I just dropped by for an estimate!"

■

Doctor (listening to his stethoscope): "Lady, has any other doctor ever treated you for this condition?"

Patient: "Never! I always pay."

■

An old man in a bus turned to the passenger next to him. "I'm begging your pardon, but do you speak Yiddish?"

The man shook his head, no, and the old man asked another passenger, who also indicated that he didn't speak Yiddish.

A third man smiled and said, "I speak Yiddish."

The old man's anxious expression disappeared. "Please then, vat time is it?"

■

Bernstein is being examined by his doctor. "So tell me how you feel? A little sluggish?"

Bernstein sighed. "If I felt that good I wouldn't be here!"

■

Zuckerman visits a famous internist who examines him thoroughly. Finally the doctor says, "Everything checks out. You look fine to me."

"But what about my headaches?"

The doctor says, "I'm not worried about your headaches."

Zuckerman says, "If you had my headaches I wouldn't worry about them either."

■

Two black chauffeurs are waiting at the railroad station for their employers to arrive. Says one, "I hear tomorrow's a big Jewish holiday. Something big, like Easter? I hear my folks talking."

The other sniffed. "Way bigger than that. Easter ain't nothin' next to Rosh Hashanah!"

"How come?"

"That's when they blow the shofar."

"Hey, those Jewish people sure know how treat their help!"

■

Saperstein returned unexpectedly from a business trip and saw a half-dressed man running out the back door. His wife, in her negligee, admitted she had been unfaithful.

"So, who was it?" he yelled. "That bastard Goldstein?"

His wife hung her head. "No it wasn't Goldstein."

"Was it Lapidus, that louse?"

"No, it wasn't Lapidus."

"I know—it must have been that *momzer*, Plotnick!"

"No, it wasn't Plotnick either."

Saperstein banged his hand on the table. "What's the matter," he yelled, "none of my friends are good enough for you?"

■

An old Jewish businessman was dozing in his train compartment when the train jerked to a stop and a smartly dressed young man bounded into the compartment.

"Sholem aleichem," he said, expecting the customary, *"Aleichem sholem"* in reply.

Instead, the elderly man sighed and said, "Listen, young fellow and it'll save time. I come from Minsk, I'm going to Pinsk, and I'm in the leather business. I sell hides, wholesale, and I have for thirty years. My name is Berkowitz, Hyman Berkowitz. I have two daughters. One is already married and the other is engaged to a rabbi. I also have two sons. Benny, the oldest, is married and in the business with me. Harold is a good student and if the damned anti-Semites at the university don't make it impossible, soon he will be a doctor.

"Also, I'm not sociable. I don't drink or play cards. And long ago I learned not to give political opinions to strangers. I think that's about it. If I've left anything out ask me quick, because I haven't slept in two nights and I'm going to take a snooze right now!"

■

Little boy to his father, "You are always talking about business. What is business?"

His father thought a few seconds and then said, "To sell something you have to someone who wants it—well, that's not business. But to sell something you don't have to someone who doesn't want it, *that's* business."

■

It came as a terrible blow to Harriet Feldman, that Milton, her solid, dependable husband of nearly forty years, had a mistress. A gossipy neighbor told her.

She accused him in a red-faced torrent of tears and re-criminations. Gently he put his arm around her and spoke softly and earnestly, explaining that successful, mature men frequently had mistresses. As a matter of fact, his partner had one for years. A mistress was no threat to their marriage, nothing could shake that. He loved Harriet more now than ever. But she must understand that as men aged they needed new sexual stimulus to keep up their pride in their masculinity. And really, the emotions were in no way involved.

And, as far as expenses was concerned, it was picayune—an apartment, a few presents, a little spending money. It was piffling to people as well-fixed as they were. She should just accept it gracefully. His partner's mistress didn't bother his partner's wife the least bit. That's the way things were today.

Harriet sniffed and sniveled and eventually accepted the situation. Time passed. One night she and Milton were at a formal charity affair when, two tables away, there sat Milton's partner with his *tsatskeleh.* "That's Sam's mistress," Milton explained. "His wife is sick and couldn't be here."

Just then a buxom brunette strode through the crowd to Sam's table and sat down. Milton said, "There's no reason why you shouldn't know. That's my mistress talking to Sam."

Harriet leaned forward and peered intently. Then she smiled and said, "You know, Milton, ours is prettier."

■

Abe was graduating from an Orthodox rabbinical college. His parents came out to the airport to meet him. He came down the ramp in his ankle-length black alpaca coat, yarmulke, beard and earlocks, and a prayer shawl. His mother looked at him adoringly and turned to his father. "Look who's here—a regular Joe College!"

■

The WASP was bragging to Schmulowitz about his blue-blooded ancestry.

"You call *yourself* an American? Why, my ancestors came over on the *Mayflower!*"

"It's lucky they did," Schmulowitz answered. "By the time my parents arrived, the immigration laws were a lot stricter!"

■

On Yom Kippur, the most holy day on the Jewish calendar, all the seats in the synagogue had been sold to ticket holders, the doors were closed, and the prayers were already in progress, when a breathless ten-year-old boy sought admission.

"You got a ticket?" asked the elderly man at the door.

"No, but my mother is very sick and I have to go in and get my father. He has to come home right away!"

The old man reflected. His instructions had been explicit: No ticket, no admission.

Finally he said, "All right, you can go get your father. But don't let me catch you praying!"

■

Because a man makes a lot of money doesn't necessarily mean he has a lot of brains. There was a man who won several million dollars in the lottery on number 14. He was asked why he picked 14. He said, "I had a dream. I saw in my dream a great big number 9, and next to it I saw a 6. So I used my head and figured 9 and 6 is 14."

■

The young optometrist asked his new boss how to price his glasses. There were no prices on the frames.

"It works like this," his boss said. "A customer comes in for new glasses. So first you examine him. Then you start showing him frames."

"But they don't have any prices on them!"

"Of course not. When the customer picks the frame he wants he'll ask you what they cost. You say, 'eight dollars.' If he doesn't object, you then add, 'And the lenses, of course, are twenty dollars.' If he still doesn't object, you tell him, 'each.'"

■

Stark naked, Shapiro is sitting in his room wearing a top hat, when his friend, Levy, walks in.

"Why are you sitting here without your clothes?"

"It doesn't matter," says Shapiro. "Nobody comes to see me."

"Then why the hat?"

"Well, maybe somebody will come."

■

The first *yenta* faces her neighbor. "You broke that pot I lent you. It's damaged so I can't use it. You got to buy me a new one!"

The second *yenta* sneers. "What are you talking? First of all it was in perfect condition when I returned it. Second, It was broken when you lent it to me. And, third, I never borrowed your lousy pot in the first place!"

■

An American Jew, traveling in Beijing, watched in wonder as the Chinese congregation, led by a pigtailed rabbi in a long, yellow silk robe conducted the Passover service. The sights and sounds were beyond his comprehension.

He rushed over to the rabbi at the conclusion of the service and, through an interpreter, explained that he, too, was Jewish.

The rabbi's eyebrows elevated. He sing-songed to the interpreter. The interpreter said, "He say, 'That's funny, you don't look Jewish.'"

■

This story about Einstein is supposed to be true. He and his wife were being guided through the Mount Wilson Observatory in California. Mrs. Einstein pointed to an enormous and complex piece of machinery and asked what it was for.

Their guide explained that the machine was used to determine the exact shape of the universe.

"Oh, that," Mrs. Einstein said. "My husband does that on the back of an old envelope."

■

Concluding his lecture at the synagogue, the astronomer told his audience, "Some of my colleagues believe that our own sun will probably die out in four, maybe five billion years."

A voice from the audience rang out, "How many years did you say?"

"Four or five billion," the astronomer answered.

"*Denks Gott!* I thought you said *million.*"

■

Two Jews planned to assassinate Hitler who was due on a certain corner precisely at noon. Guns hidden under their coats, they waited for him. Twelve o'clock came and went. Twelve-thirty. Still no Hitler. Their hope faded. *"Oy!"* said one of them. "I hope nothing's happened to him!"

■

Gottlieb lay dying. Feebly he beckoned to his wife. "Call a priest," he said. "Tell him I want to convert."

"Sydney, what are you saying? All your life you've been an Orthodox Jew. What are you saying? You want to convert?"

He wheezed, "Better one of them should die than one of us."

■

Two huge Martian spaceships landed midday in the midst of the bustling downtown shopping section.

Screaming with terror at the sight of the eight-foot, three-armed Martians, storekeepers and shoppers fled wildly in every direction. All but Sam and Abe, who were engrossed in putting the finishing touches on the windows of their men's wear "Grand Opening" sale.

Then, suddenly, from his perch on the top of the ladder, Sam saw the Martians lumbering toward them. "Abe! Abe!" he screamed. "Quick, before it's too late! Take down the 'Free Alterations' sign."

■

Seventy-year-old Sussman was explaining the peculiarities of his sex life to his doctor. "You wouldn't believe this, doctor, but it's absolutely true. The first time I make love to my wife I get cold, freezing cold. I shiver and my teeth chatter. But then, the second time, I get burning hot. I'm sweating all over. I'm running a temperature. What's with me? The first time cold, the second time hot."

The doctor examined him thoroughly and could find nothing amiss. "Perhaps it has something to do with your wife's metabolism. Have her come see me."

Sadie arrived the next day and the doctor gave her Sussman's story. She laughed.

"A big *tsimmes* over nothing. You don't have to examine me. It's simple, a child could understand. The first time it's February. It's cold, so he shivers. But the second time it's August. It's hot, so he perspires."

■

Epstein finally managed an appointment with the great J. P. Morgan for the purpose of getting backing for his latest boon to humanity.

"Tell me quickly," Morgan said. "I have no time to waste."

Epstein took a small bottle from his briefcase. "We got here the basis of a revolution in personal hygiene. Something every woman will want—a deodorant that makes women smell like oranges. Here, smell."

"Rubbish," said Morgan. "This is supposed to make millions? Who the hell wants to smell like an orange? Like flowers, maybe, or ocean breezes or pine trees. But oranges? Get out of here!"

Six months passed. Epstein was getting into his Mercedes when Morgan's stretch limo pulled up and Morgan stuck his head out. Epstein waved grandly.

Morgan smiled ruefully. "Well, Epstein, it looks like you were right and I was wrong. So your invention was a success. Congratulations!"

Epstein look puzzled. "Which invention was that?"

"Your deodorant that made women smell like oranges," Morgan said.

"Oh, that. No, you were right, J. P. It didn't go. But I reversed the formula and made a fortune."

"Reversed it? What do you mean?"

"Now it makes oranges smell like a woman and I can't make enough of it."

■ ■ ■

A current popular Yiddish expression is being applied to just about everything: *ongepotchket*. Moe Bronfman used it often. It has a wide variety of meanings, including:

- Cluttered
- Disordered
- Littered
- Muddled

- Confused
- Sloppy
- Too ornate
- Overdone

■

With three good seasons under his belt, Moe had redecorated his office with a tremendous (six by nine feet) all-white, rough-surfaced canvas with a nickel-size black dot in the lower left-hand corner.

Now he returned to the gallery that had sold it to him, to buy another, just as "provocative." All his customers had been intrigued by it and now considered Moe a connoisseur.

"Maybe you got another by Pishteppel?" he asked the dealer.

The dealer had one and assured him that it would arouse just as much interest as the first. In it came, again a huge, white, rough-surfaced canvas devoid of any decoration but *two* black dots in the corner.

Bronfman rose, closed one eye, and squinted over his thumb. He moved toward the canvas and backed away from it. He canted his head left and right. Then he shook his head.

"Nah, not for me. It lacks the classic simplicity of the first one. It's too *ongepotchket!*"

■   ■   ■

A Chasidic Jew from Brooklyn was invited to his nephew's graduation from the University of Mississippi. He took the train down and emerged dusty and travel-worn, tall and gaunt in his flat-brimmed beaver hat; long, black gabardine coat; full beard; long, unshorn ear ringlets; soft high-button shoes; and dangling prayer shawl.

There was no cab at the station but a small black boy assured him that it was only a short walk to the university. He started shuffling up the road. The little boy followed. Other little black boys joined the first, then three curious dogs and a little girl. Soon it was a small parade. The Chasid stopped and turned to his followers. "Vat's de mattuh? You never seen a Yankee before?"

A kosher poultry market is much more than merely a place to buy fowl. It is the battleground for an endless war of wits between the customers and the butcher. Jewish housewives don't simply buy chickens, they negotiate. Between them and the butcher is an uneasy armed truce. They thoroughly distrust each other.

A grim housewife asks the butcher, "You got for me a *good* chicken?"

Silent and frowning, implying by his expression that he doesn't carry anything *but* good chickens, he pulls a scrawny, blueish fowl from a hook in back of him and slams it down on the counter.

She grabs the bird by the neck, lifts each bony wing, and sniffs violently underneath. Then she inserts an exploratory finger into the body cavity and sniffs there as well. She pinches the skin and stretches it. Then she bangs the chicken on the counter, her nose wrinkled in disgust. "You call *this* a chicken?"

"Lady," the butcher answers, "tell me something. Could you pass an inspection like that?"

■

Ben and Sarah had made their little pile the hard way, working together in a little Mom 'n' Pop candy store, then a larger store, then a small chain of stores. But in their upward climb there had been no time for culture.

Now they were rich and retired in a wealthy community where they attached themselves to an educated group interested in books, music, art, and the theater. But at the many dinners when their new friends talked of these things, they were painfully quiet, ashamed of their ignorance.

Suddenly one night at a neighbor's when the talk turned to music and composers, Sarah startled everyone by saying, "It's funny you should mention Mozart. Only the other day I saw him in Chicago."

There was an appalled silence. Then a chilly voice asked, "Whom did you see?"

"Mozart, on the number 34 bus going to the Art Institute."

There was another profound silence before conversation

resumed. Ben was mortified and a few minutes later insisted that they had to leave.

In the car he turned furiously to Sarah. "What the hell did you tell them a thing like that for and show your ignorance?"

"But it's the truth. Harry Mozart *was* on the number 34 bus!"

Ben waved his hand impatiently. "Yeah, yeah. But, dope, everyone knows the number 34 bus goes to Oak Street Beach and not to the Art Institute!"

■

Everyone knew that Sussman was the richest man in Cedarhurst, with the grandest house, the biggest boat, and the most oceanfront property. His computer-software business had made him millions. But he never contributed to charity and was completely antisocial. No one had ever seen the inside of his mansion. And all his shopping in town was done by his chauffeur in his white Rolls-Royce.

But now, their hearts pounding, the committee for building the new synagogue stood in his sumptuous foyer awaiting Sussman.

He was surprisingly gracious and listened courteously enough as the chairman recited his carefully rehearsed appeal. The Jewish community was growing and needed a new building. It was only through the generosity of leaders like himself that the synagogue and Hebrew school would be possible. Could they depend on a generous contribution?

Sussman nodded and looked intently at his polished fingernails. "I'm afraid there are a few things about me that you don't know. Sit down, please, and I'll tell you."

"I have an older brother, Barry, who's in a mental institution. He's been there nearly twenty years and he'll never get any better. He could live another twenty, thirty years. Do you have any idea what that costs?"

"Then there's Tilly, my younger sister, with arthritis so bad she's twisted like a pretzel and can't work. She's a widow with four children to raise. You don't have the faintest idea how much money that takes."

"And my mother, she's eighty-six, deaf, nearly blind, and

incontinent, with nurses around the clock. Her nursing-home bill comes to over forty thousand a year."

"And, last, there's Yetta, my older sister. She's got cancer, a long, slow kind. One operation after another, radium, chemo-therapy, expensive medicines, doctors, clinics, lab fees, no end."

"Now, gentlemen, if they can't get a goddamn cent out of me, what the hell chance do you think your lousy synagogue has?"

■

Feinstein, a very religious old man, had spent several days seeking a suitable retirement home. It must be not only strictly kosher, but observe all the Jewish holidays and have a resident rabbi.

Now the director of Flugelman's Retirement Home was showing him around.

"Let me call your attention to the generous size of your room and bath and the absolutely soundproof walls and floors. Nothing will disturb your peace and quiet. Notice also the large TV and the VCR, as well as the luxurious wall-to-wall carpeting."

Feinstein was nearly sold, but he wanted to be absolutely certain that Flugelman's was for him. A warning bell rang. Something very important was missing.

He opened the door and looked out into the hall. Sure enough, he was right. There was no *mezuzah* (the tiny box affixed to the right side of a Jewish doorway containing verses of Deuteronomy printed on parchment)! "So where's the *mezuzah*, if you're so very *frum*?"

The director smiled and pointed heavenward. "You're dealing with twentieth-century Judaism here, Mr. Feinstein. Every apartment is directly connected to a master *mezuzah* on the roof!"

■

The typical Jewish mother is supposed to be happy only when there is something to be unhappy about. Expressions of hurt and dissatisfaction are as normal as breathing. She is forever on the defensive against some slight to her feelings.

Typical is this mother who gave her successful lawyer son two silk ties for his birthday—one red, the other blue.

Knowing that his mother was coming for dinner, he dutifully put on the blue tie. Mother arrived. She kissed her son and then recoiled, a look of pain on her face.

"What's the matter, you don't like the red one?"

■

Sophie Nachman goes to her neighborhood gypsy fortune-teller. "Tell me, fortune-teller, can you put me in touch with my dear, departed grandmother?"

"She died? When was that?"

"Almost a month ago. There is nothing in the world I want so much as to hear her dear voice once again. Can you get in touch with her in the Great Beyond?"

"You got ten dollars?"

"Yes."

"Then I'll get right in touch with her....Hello, out there, hello. Hello, Grandmother....Your beloved granddaughter wants to speak to you. Can you hear me?"

(Faint, quavery voice) "Hello, Granddaughter, is that really you?"

"Yes, Grandmother, it is! I miss you so much. Tell me, how are you?"

"I'm just fine, not a thing to complain."

"Tell me, Grandmother, one thing I must know about you. When did you learn to speak English?"

■

The surly drunk lurched into the El-Al airliner and sat down heavily, bumping roughly against the young woman in the seat next to him. Cradled in her arms was a tiny sleeping infant who awoke at the rough contact and started to cry.

"Watch what you're doing, please! You already upset my baby!" she said.

The man glanced at her through red, heavy-lidded eyes and leaned toward the infant. "So you got a baby, huh?" he asked stupidly. "What am I supposed to do, stop breathing, just because you got a baby?"

She glared at him and pulled the baby's blankets tighter around him. As she did, his cap fell off revealing a tiny, hairless, wrinkled scalp; red, wizened features; tiny, squinty eyes, and a drooling, open, toothless mouth.

The drunk uttered a braying laugh which infuriated the mother.

"A living doll!" he said sarcastically. The woman yelled and berated the drunk, the baby howled, and the short, plump Israeli hostess came running to quell the disturbance.

"This man insulted me and my baby. He's drunk and disgusting. I want my seat changed immediately! Immediately, do you understand!"

"Don't get yourself excited," the hostess said. "I got no empty seat to give you. This is all just a misunderstanding. I'll bring this gentleman some black coffee to straighten him out and some nice warm milk for you so you'll relax."

Then she leaned over the red-faced screaming infant. "And a banana for your monkey!"

■

Gasping and wheezing, Liebowitz is dying. His son Merwin, from California, is at his bedside holding his hand. The old man coughs and says, "This is the end!"

"No, Papa," Merwin says, "it's not the end, don't be foolish."

"Merwin, whom are you kidding? This is the end and we both know it. Only one thing I want more than anything in the world before I go."

"Anything, Papa, anything you want. What can I bring you?"

"Bring me, please, for my last pleasure, a piece of your mama's delicious apple strudel. I can smell it now. She just baked it."

Merwin rushes out and returns two minutes later, empty-handed, his face distressed.

Liebowitz gasps, "The strudel, where's the strudel?"

Merwin sighs. "I'm sorry, Papa. Mama says you can't have it. It's for after the funeral!"

■

First alrightnik: "I understand you got to Rome?"
Second ditto: "But of course, what then?"
First: "Well, what did you think of the Colosseum?"
Second: "Oh, it's all right, if you like modern."

■

Teenage movie critic reporting to a friend: "It's a lousy movie. Don't fail to miss it if you can."

■

Diner: "You call this meat?"
Waiter: "What's wrong with it?"
Diner: "Wrong? It tastes funny."
Waiter: "So laugh!"

The pet-shop owner said, "Rabbi, it's lucky you came in. It must be fate. A customer of mine, a very holy man, spent two years training this parrot just before he died. This is a truly religious bird. But, well, see for yourself."

He whisked the cover off a large cage in which a brilliant green parrot sat on a perch, a long string dangling from each leg.

"Let me show you now. Just reach in and pull a string."

The rabbi did and the bird tucked that leg up into its feathers and proceeded to squawk the Ten Commandments. The rabbi exclaimed, "That is a miracle. I never heard anything like it."

The store owner said, "Now pull the other string." The rabbi did and the bird screeched out a recognizable rendition of "Kol Nidre."

"Why—why—" stuttered the rabbi, "a marvel of piety. But what would happen if I pulled both strings at once?"

The bird stuck its beak out between the wires of the cage and glared at him. "I'd fall flat on my ass, you dumb jerk. What do you think!"

■

Levine, a horseplayer, dreamed up an idea how to make a killing. He spent nearly a year training his parrot, Velvel, to recite the Rosh Hashanah service. The bird was quick and soon was letter perfect. Just before the holidays Levine fitted him with a little yarmulke and took the bird to his men's club, where he announced that Velvel could conduct all the prayers without a single mistake.

The bird sat absolutely still and the men roared in derision. But Levine was sure of his ground, he knew what Velvel could do. "I'll bet each of you twenty bucks that he does it." The bird fluttered nervously and made not a sound. One by one the men put up their money and piled it on a table.

"Okay, Velvel, let 'em have it," said the cocksure Levine. The bird remained absolutely silent and, after twenty minutes of frenzied coaxing, Levine had to pay off.

On the way home in his car Levine yanked the cover off the cage. "You lousy bird! You know what you cost me, you little stinker? Besides making me look like a jerk. You know the service perfectly. Why didn't you open your beak? I ought to wring your neck, that's what!"

"You *are* a jerk," squawked Velvel. "I'm on your side but you're too dumb to know it. Did you ever stop to think what odds we can get on Yom Kippur?"

■

Sam had been very uncomfortable for days, his bowels tied in a knot. He didn't like to bother his wife with such things, but finally he confessed why he had been so glum.

"We'll go to the doctor," she said, and they did.

The doctor was sympathetic and gave Sam a small bottle of suppositories. "Just take one of these rectally, twice a day, and you'll be okay."

Outside the doctor's office Sam and Sarah looked at each other blankly. "Rectally?" he asked. "What's rectally?"

She shrugged, "Who knows? Fancy doctor language. How do you always take medicine? You swallow. So wash one down with a glass of tea."

He did and waited and waited and waited. So that night he swallowed another, following Sarah's suggestion to break it up real small.

He repeated the process next day. No relief. Acutely uncomfortable, he stormed into the doctor's office and complained that the medication was no good.

"You followed my instructions?" the doctor asked.

"Of course, in the morning and at night."

"You took them rectally?"

"Rectally-schmectally, for all the good they did, I might just as well have shoved them up my ass!"

■

Father Flannigan and Rabbi Markowitz were friends and neighbors. Their middle-class congregations were spread out over many miles so that each needed a car. But money was short. They discussed the problem candidly and finally came to the inspired conclusion that they share one. So they bought a small Toyota and worked out a schedule of alternate use.

Next morning Rabbi Markowitz was disturbed to see Father Flannigan walking around the car intoning in Latin and splashing holy water on it from a censer. It seemed an unfair advantage. Certainly the car was half-Jewish. What to do?

Next day the good father was surprised to see the rabbi sprawled under the rear bumper, hacksaw in hand, cutting two inches off the exhaust pipe.

■

When her husband died, Mrs. Friedman had no end of trouble with Medicare, the hospital, the doctors, the undertaker, and relations. Worst of all was the insurance company. But finally she got her check, and the agent, an old friend, tried to cheer her by telling her all the pleasant things she could do with the money.

"Oh, I don't know," Mrs. Friedman sighed. "I've had so much trouble with everything that there are times when I wish Benny never got hit by that truck."

■

Said one proud Jewish mother to her dearest friend, "So how is your son, Seymour, the doctor, doing in Glenview these days?"

"Wonderful, just wonderful. His practice has grown like crazy. He's making so much money that he doesn't have to operate on every patient anymore."

■

The old man had an ugly rash on his hands. He went in to see Doctor Cowlan, who had just recently hung out his shingle.

He examined the old man's hands under a magnifying glass and took X rays. Then he referred to two large medical tomes and shook his head.

"Tell me," he asked the old man, "have you ever had this before?"

"Yeah, doc. Years ago."

"Well," diagnosed the shrewd young medico, "you sure have it again!"

■

Lawyer: "You want me to make out a new will, Bronfman? Leaving everything to the family—same as before?"

Bronfman: "Absolutely not. They're not getting a plugged nickel. My entire estate goes to the doctor who saves my life."

■

The doctor told Miller, a condominium tycoon, that he needed an operation. He said, "Do you want a local anesthetic?"

Miller shook his head. "Let's not pinch pennies, doc, get the best. Use imported."

■

J. P. Morgan looked at his old friend Lapidus who, once again, wanted financing for a great new invention.

"I don't understand what you're selling. You say it's an *invisible* deodorant? What good is that?"

Lapidus said, "It's miraculous. As soon as you put it on, you disappear so that no one can tell where the smell's coming from."

■

The little compact car smashed into the rear of Blumberg's Cadillac as he made a left turn.

The driver of the little car was furious. "Why the hell didn't you put out your hand?"

"What's the point?" shrugged Blumberg. "If you can't see my Cadillac, how could you see my hand?"

■

Tevye's new helper was from Minsk and, as a city boy, didn't know much about cows. He had been milking for nearly an hour when Tevye stopped by to see how he was doing. To the dairyman's surprise the helper was feeding the cow with milk.

"What in the name of the Almighty, blessed be His name, do you think you are doing?"

"The cow put its dirty tail in the pail, so I'm running the milk through her again."

■

Rosenfeld returned to his native shtetl after many years in America. To his delight, his old rabbi was still alive and he went to see him.

"I hope you've been a good Jew," the old man said, "wherever you were."

"Indeed I was, rabbi, hard as it often was to make a living. I lied, I robbed, I took the Lord's name in vain. I ate trayf food, and had many women. But never, not even for one second, did I ever forget the religion I was brought up in."

■

An elderly Jewish woman was walking along Delancey Street when a "flasher" accosted her and opened his shabby raincoat. She stared at him for a moment and then said, "Hmmm, you call *that* a lining?"

■

A father is helping his son with his homework.

Son: "Hey, Pop, how would you define electronics?"
Father: "Electronics, sorry I don't know much about electronics."
Son: "How does gasoline make a car engine go?"
Father: "I'm afraid gas engines are Greek to me."
Son: "What do they mean by hydrostatic pressure?"
Father: "Sounds like something that comes out of a hydrant. We didn't have that when I was a boy."
Son: "How many genes does a human being have?"
Father: "Oh, lots and lots. I forget the exact number."
Son: "Gee, Pop, I'm sorry I'm making such a pest of myself."
Father: "Not at all. Glad to help. If you don't ask questions you'll never learn anything."

■

Schmerl, the fancy pastry baker, boasted that he could make any kind of fancy cake for any occasion. Nothing was too unusual or too complicated.

A man came into his shop. He wanted a very special mocha creme layer cake. "I know I'm very fussy," he said, "but I want this cake exactly the way I want it and price is no object, okay?"

merl. "I'll write down everything and read it
e can be no mistake."

vith it has to be in the shape of an hourglass,
and with seven layers of alternating whipped
illing. And on top there must be three dozen
rosettes in pink icing. And, oh, the last thing, it has to be one
hundred percent absolutely kosher. Now, can you do it?"

"Of course I can do it, and I'll have my uncle, the rabbi,
supervise every step in its production. Now is that all you want?"

"Oh no. I told you this was a very special cake. I want 'Happy
Birthday Lester Sonenshine' in pink script letters exactly three
inches high on top. Are you sure you can do it?"

"Yes, but I'll need two days."

"Okay," said the man. "Timing is important. I'll be in for it at
three o'clock, sharp, Thursday."

He arrived promptly at that time and Schmerl wheeled in his
triumph. "There, by God. I told you I could make it and there it
is! A masterpiece if I say so myself."

The customer looked at it, shook his head, and groaned.
"Oh, no! You didn't get the spirit of it at all! I ordered script
letters and not block letters. I can't use that."

"Look, mister." Schmerl said, seeing his two-hundred-dollar-
order vanishing. "it's easy to fix. Come back in an hour and I'll
have it all relettered."

The man agreed, walked out, and returned in exactly an
hour. "Marvelous!" he exclaimed. "Now you've got it exactly
right. A masterpiece! Everything I'd hoped for."

"Thank heaven," said Schmerl. "Now tell me where do you
want it delivered?"

"Delivered?" said the man. "I don't want it delivered anywhere. "I'll eat it right here."

■

"My wife is driving me absolutely crazy," Horowitz told his
friend. "She has absolutely the world's worst memory."

"You mean," said his sympathetic friend, "that she can't
remember anything?"

"Hell no! Just the opposite, damn it. She remembers
everything."

Blitzstein was walking in the park with fellow pet lover Hymowitz, who had his peppy young Airedale on a leash. Blitzstein watched enviously. Hymowitz said, "You miss your dog, huh? You look unhappy."

Blitzstein's eyes filled with tears. "I had to shoot my dog!"

"Why, was he mad?"

"He wasn't exactly pleased about it."

■

Two Miami Mamas were comparing notes on their recent vacations. The first bragged about their luxurious stay in Hawaii and asked her friend where she had been.

She preened. "*We* went to Majorca!

"Majorca? Where's that?"

"I don't know. We flew."

■

White with rage, Nudelman leaped up from the card table. "Stop the game!" he yelled. "Levy's cheating!"

"How do you know?"

"He's not playing the hand I dealt him!"

■

Fannie Frumpkin had the grandfather of all colds. It lingered for weeks and simply wouldn't go away despite all the expensive medication her doctor prescribed.

"Oh, doctor," she groaned, "isn't there *something* you can do?"

"Yes, there is," he said. "It's drastic but I know it will work. Go home and take a bath, as hot as you can take it. Then, without drying yourself, stand in front of an open window, absolutely naked, where there's a strong draft."

"Will that cure me?" Fannie asked.

"No, it won't. But it'll give you pneumonia and we know how to cure pneumonia."

■

"You're doing marvelous," Hartman said to his partner. "I can't believe you've been playing golf for only a month!"

"That's all. But of course it took me four years to learn."

Johnny Jepkowitz was one of the world's great jockeys. But this time he came in dead last.

The horse's owner groaned. "Johnny, *last?* Couldn't you have gone any faster?"

"Sure I could, a lot faster. But you know we're supposed to stay with the horse."

■

A quick-witted lawyer rushed out of the crowd and picked up the little old lady who had just been knocked down by a taxi. "Here's my card, lady," he said. "Just leave it to me. I'll get you damages."

"Damages?" she yelled. "Who wants damages? Damages I got. What I need is repairs!"

■

Papa Melnick was afraid that his son across the ocean in New York might be forgetting his religion among the distractions of the big city. So he cabled him at the Waldorf, "Yom Kippur starts tomorrow."

Young Melnick immediately called his bookie. "I never heard of the nag, myself. But if my father thinks he's worth cabling about, put a hundred on the nose for me."

■

Old Hartman told his doctor that he wanted his sex lowered.

"Lowered?" said the doctor. "That's a new one on me. What do you mean 'lowered'? Most guys your age want to be able to get it up."

Hartman sighed. "No, I want it lowered. Right now it's all in my head. I want it lowered, to my crotch, where it belongs."

■

The TV industry conducted a year-long survey to find out exactly what the American viewers most wanted to see. The results were surprising and the industry decided not to reveal its findings: People enjoyed sitting in the dark and would rather look at most anything rather than at each other!

The Bible is hardly the place to find a description of a hot rod. But according to The Song of Solomon, no Harlem vice lord had fancier "wheels" than the king himself:

> King Solomon made himself a chariot of the wood of Lebanon. He made the pillars thereof of silver, the bottom thereof of gold, the covering of it purple, the midst thereof being paved with love, for the daughters of Jerusalem.

■

One of the first things Jewish immigrant couples did after their marriage was to have their bridal portrait taken. Props were very important, as they indicated status to the folks in the old country. So the photographer provided jewelry, eyeglasses, and pencils; the last two indicating education, the ability to read and write.

The standard pose for newlyweds, taken the morning after their wedding, was for the groom to be seated, grimly staring straight ahead, with the bride standing erect at his side.

This was no perversion of manners. Tittering friends and relatives always confided that it was because the groom was too exhausted to stand and the bride too sore to sit down.

■

Abramowitz, a wealthy pants manufacturer, was suspicious of the motives of the young man who wanted to marry his daughter. "I wonder if you'd be so eager to marry Hannah if I didn't have a cent to my name?"

"I'd love her more than ever," vowed the suitor. "Because then she would have to depend entirely on me."

"Get out," growled Abramowitz, "we've got enough idiots in the family already!"

■

The floor nurse at Evanston Hospital answered the phone. A man's voice asked how Mr. Fleischman was doing. Fleischman in room 139.

"Just fine," she said. "He's coming along nicely. I believe

they're going to let him go home tomorrow. Whom should I say called?"

The voice chuckled. "This is Fleischman, himself. Those doctors wouldn't tell me a damned thing."

■

Car buff Fidelman returned to his parked Mercedes to find the left front fender crumpled and a note under his windshield wiper!

"The people who saw me back into your car are watching me write this note. They think I'm leaving my name and address and phone so you can contact me and send me the repair bill. Boy, are they naïve!"

■

The first Jewish astronaut was just about to board his spaceship when a reporter nabbed him. "Tell me, Mr. Levy, what are you thinking when you're all strapped in and waiting for blast-off?"

"Well, I can never forget that I'm sitting in the middle of about a hundred thousand parts—all supplied by the lowest bidder."

■

A recent visit by the Pope, resplendent in an embroidered white yarmulke (you can bet he doesn't call it that), reminded us that, contrary to its use in the synagogue, the skullcap is now a fashion item. None of the following is invented: There are Ivy League yarmulkes in over a dozen different designs including two-tones and plaids; reds, grays, and blacks. They can be with initials (either script or block letters), fraternity or other organization symbols, embroidered, and with satin linings.

Wonder if the Pope's high, pointed hat with the two streamers will ever be as popular with non-Catholics?

A famous rabbi's six-year-old daughter was drawing pictures with her crayons. Her mother asked whose picture she was drawing.

"God's," she answered unhesitatingly.

"But, darling," her mother said, "nobody knows how God looks."

The daughter said, "They will when I'm finished."

■

Two competitive traveling salesmen met one morning outside an inn. The first asked, "*Nu*, so where are you going now?"

The second hesitated for just a second and then said, "I'm going to Minsk."

"For shame," said the first. "When you tell me you're going to Minsk, you really want me to believe you're going to Pinsk. But you didn't fool me. I happen to know that you *are* going to Minsk. So what are you lying for?"

■

A poor Talmudic scholar was working on his Torah commentary with total concentration. The town's richest man scoffed. "What a waste of energy! Stop writing, it won't get you anywhere."

The scholar wiped his tearing eyes. "And if I stopped writing—it would get me somewhere?"

■

Sweating and grunting, the little shtetl tradesman plunked an immense, heavy package on the post-office counter. The clerk put it on the scales. "It's too heavy," he said. "It needs more stamps."

"And if I put on more stamps," asked the man, "that'll make it lighter?"

■

An old Jewish innkeeper was discussing the tricks of the trade with a friend. "I rarely will sell a man a *shnaps* on credit. But when I do I charge double."

"I, on the other hand," said his friend, "always charge *less* than for cash."

"What the devil's the sense in that?"

"Very simple, if a man doesn't pay on credit it makes my loss that much less."

■

A farmer was driving his wagon to market when he spied a beggar limping along with a heavy pack on his back. Feeling sorry for him, the farmer offered the beggar a ride.

They drove on in silence until the farmer saw that the beggar still had the pack on his shoulders. "Why don't you put it down?" he asked the man in surprise.

"Bless you," said the beggar, "you've done enough already carrying me. Why should I burden your horse with my pack besides?"

■

The filthy, tattered beggar, starving, stood in the rich man's doorway and begged for help.

The rich man sighed in pity. "Master of the Universe, *look* at this poor creature! His toes are sticking out of his shoes. His pants are ripped and threadbare. He looks and smells as if he hasn't washed or shaved in weeks. You alone know when he had his last decent meal. It is breaking my heart just to look at him! I can't stand such misery.

"O Master of the Universe, give me strength to throw the bum out!"

■

The wise men came from miles around to see the simple shepherd who could do instant counting of vast sums in his head. Faster than they could write the figures down, he could look at any flock of sheep and say, practically instantly, how many there were—a hundred, five hundred, a thousand— more. It did not matter—he was always right. The owners of the sheep always substantiated his count.

Now the oldest of the wise men asked the young shepherd how he did it. Was such a lightning brain a gift from God?

The youth smiled sweetly and shook his head. No, nothing like that, really. It was a simple trick: All he did was count the legs and divide by four.

A Polish-Jewish peddler is traveling in a first-class train compartment. The kindhearted conductor had allowed him there because it was the last empty compartment on the train. The peddler looks around in awed appreciation at the rich upholstery and deluxe fittings and proceeds to make himself comfortable—unbuttoning his coat, removing his shoes, throwing his head back, and putting his feet up on the opposite seat.

Suddenly the door is flung open and a military-looking gentleman wearing a rich-looking greatcoat with a fur collar and a tall Astrakhan hat enters and seats himself.

The peddler immediately sits up, takes his feet off the seat, puts his shoes on, combs his hair and beard with his fingers, and sits primly erect. The stranger sits in silence doing some figures in a handsome notebook he has taken from his pocket. Suddenly he says, "Pardon me, but do you know when Yom Kippur is this year?"

"Ahhh," says the peddler, opening his collar, removing his shoes, and elevating his feet again.

■

It was Czarist Russia and the lord of the manor was furious at Malkin, his tollgate keeper, who had been caught letting his friends through the gate free. The lord's punishment was severe and ingenious: Either Malkin would teach a dog, which the lord would supply, to read prayers aloud in Hebrew from the Holy Scroll, or Malkin would be beheaded.

Malkin agreed that the dog would read the prayers, but it would take a little education. Was the lord's dog very intelligent?

"Of course my dog is intelligent, you stupid Jew!" roared the lord.

"Then" said Malkin, "I can teach him to pray in six months rather than the year it would normally take."

The lord released him and Malkin departed with the mongrel under his arm.

"*Oy vay!*" wailed his wife. "Why did you ever make such a crazy agreement? Even the most Holy of Holy Ones, blessed be His name, cannot make a dog speak, much less read prayers aloud in Hebrew. You will be killed!"

Malkin shrugged. "Maybe not. If I refused this impossible

task he would have killed me on the spot. Now I have six months, and there are four possibilities. *One*, that there will be a miracle and the dog will read and pray aloud in Hebrew. *Two*, in six months the dog could die. *Three*, in that time the lord could die. *Four*, I could die. Six months is a long time."

Then he grinned. "But should we all be alive and well around the hundred and eightieth day, I will say Kaddish for the animal."

■

Mrs. Plotkin, a *zaftig* 180 pounds, brings home a new dress, size ten. Along with it is a whale-boned corset supposed to compress her so that she can get into it.

She calls her husband in to approve the dress and the undergarment. He takes it in his hand and shakes his head. "It will do as much good *vi a toyten bankes!*"*

■

Seventh Avenue boss: "Look, Hymie, I'd like to help you out. But it wouldn't be fair. If I let you take off a half day, I'd have to do it for everyone else in the shop whose wife gave birth to triplets."

■

The booking agent wasn't enthusiastic. He told the young man, "Yeah, Goldman, it's unusual to hear a poodle talk. A good novelty act, for a short time. But if you think anybody's going to give you a million bucks for a talking dog, you're crazy! Who'd pay it?"

"Nobody," agreed Goldman, "but I bet I can find a half-dozen dog-food manufacturers who'll pay me a million just to keep him quiet!"

---

*Prior to the twentieth century "cupping" was the accepted way of reducing the fever of a sick person. In Yiddish, the expression *bankes* (from the Slavic) meant the cups used for bleeding the sick. *Toyten* was from the German *tod*, "dead." The whole expression was *"Es vet helfen vi a toyten bankes,"* literally: It's as much use as cupping a corpse.

Lee Hershkowitz was willing to admit that he knew more about horse racing than anyone else in the theater. He came back from Aqueduct one day practically glowing.

He told his friends at Sardi's, "Today was my day. I licked them! In the first race, the second race, the third race, the fourth race, the fifth and the sixth. And, if I'd have had a dime left, I would have licked them in the seventh race, too."

■

Just before he was to make the keynote speech at the big UJA banquet, Kravitz discovered that his top denture had split. He whispered to the toastmaster that he would have to cancel his talk.

"Absolutely not!" said the toastmaster. "Here's a spare I have in my pocket."

Like magic, he produced the plate, which, unfortunately, didn't fit. Miraculously, he produced a second, which also didn't fit. And then, a third—which fit well enough.

At the conclusion of his speech the grateful Kravitz turned to the toastmaster.

"I don't know how I can thank you enough. It sure was lucky for me that you happened to be a dentist."

"Glad to help," said the toastmaster, "but I'm not a dentist, I'm an undertaker."

■

A Jewish philosopher was about to bite into a delicious *kugel* (pudding) when one of his disciples asked why it was called a *kugel*.

The philosopher said, "It's obvious. It's shaped like a *kugel*. It's sweet like a *kugel*, isn't it? It's thick like a *kugel*, isn't it? And it tastes like a *kugel*. So why shouldn't we call it *kugel*?"

■

Two little boys are walking to school. The Catholic boy says to his Jewish schoolmate, "My priest is smarter than your rabbi. He knows lots more."

The Jewish boy said, "He should, you *tell* him everything."

A Jewish shopkeeper walked past a Czarist officer in the street. The officer yelled at the Jew for not doffing his hat as required by law. "Lousy Jew," he shouted, "your insolence is insufferable. Where are you from?"

"From Odessa," the Jew answered humbly.

"What about your hat?"

"Also from Odessa," answered the Jew.

■

A Jewish businessman on a local southern board of education saw that he, alone, intended to follow the new desegregation laws.

A fellow board member asked him, "You have a daughter, don't you, Levy?'

"Yes, I do."

"And do you propose to let her go to school with the nigras?"

"I intend to follow the law," Levy said.

"Then would you let her marry a nigra?"

"Mister, I wouldn't let her marry any of you *goyim!*"

■

A shipwrecked Jew was rescued after many years on a tiny South Pacific island. Resourceful and energetic, he had done much to improve his lot—including building a hut, putting in crops and irrigation ditches and a narrow road. At the end of the road were two small buildings. "Those," he told his rescuers, "are synagogues."

"But why two? You are all alone here."

"Yes, of course. But this one, here, is where I pray, and the other I wouldn't go into if you paid me."

■

Silverman was retiring early from his women's coat-manufacturing business and giving his son all the rules for success. "Sol, I'm turning the whole thing over to you. It's a business that has made me a good living. And if you run it right it'll do the same for you.

"Just follow my principles and you'll never go wrong. Just two principles: honesty and wisdom. Nothing is more important than honesty. When you promise to deliver goods February fifteenth you deliver them February fifteenth—no matter what. Strikes, fires, floods even, you deliver February fifteenth."

"Okay, Pop, I get it. But where does wisdom come in?"

"Wisdom means, dummy, who said you should promise?"

■

The buyer for a Chicago women's sportswear chain reordered a consignment of separates from a New York manufacturer. Instead of the garments he got a fax: "Sorry, cannot fill order until previous order is paid for."

Sadly, the buyer for the chain replied: "Please cancel order. We cannot wait that long."

■

Mrs. Isaac's house was freshly painted inside and looked beautiful. She complimented the old man who had done the job. He finished late and agreed to pick up all his things in the morning.

Unfortunately, Mr. Isaacs got into bed that night, touched the still damp wall, and caused a big smear. His wife told him not to fret, that the painter was coming in the morning and she would have him touch it up.

Next morning the old painter arrived while Mrs. Isaacs was still in bed, upstairs.

"Oh, painter," she called, "please come up to the bedroom. I want to show you where my husband put his hand last night."

"Thanks, lady," said the old man, "but I got a big day ahead of me. If it's all the same to you, I'll settle for a nice cup of coffee."

■

A seventy-eight-old man whose second wife had just died, fell in love with her twenty-year-old nurse and wanted to marry her. But, because he was cautious, he decided to get his rabbi's opinion first.

The rabbi said, "It's an unusual situation, but if your doctor says you're okay, I can't find any religious reason to say no.

But—and here he winked broadly—"my advice also is that you should take in a boarder."

The old man agreed and married the girl. Some months later he ran into the rabbi, who asked how he was getting along.

"No complaints, rabbi, no complaints."

"And how is the wife?"

"God be praised, she's pregnant."

The rabbi smiled a knowing smile.

"And how's the boarder?"

"She's pregnant too!"

■

Groucho Marx, a veritable fountainhead of ad libs, never outdid his answer to a gruff customs guard who questioned him as he was returning from Caliente.

"What's your name?" barked the guard.

"Groucho Marx," he said, certain the guard had surely recognized him.

"What's your nationality?"

"American."

"What's your occupation?"

Groucho looked cautiously to his right and then to his left and held his hand up to the side of his mouth, "Smuggler!"

■

Because Mayor Daley played no favorites, a famous and beloved rabbi and an equally well-known and popular Catholic priest, sat side by side at a big civic banquet.

The priest chuckled when they were served baked Virginia ham.

"Rabbi Levy, when are you going to become liberal enough to eat ham?"

The rabbi smiled as the waiter set his special order of baked fish in front of him. "At your wedding, Father Callahan," said the rabbi.

■

Israel Polansky, a friendless, penniless Jewish immigrant, newly arrived, was faced with the immediate problem of earning a living. He was likable and soon made friends with other East Side New York Jews who got together and proposed him for the job of *shammes* (janitor) of a small synagogue on Rivington Street.

But, since he was illiterate, he couldn't fill out the job application. He was turned down; because the *shammes* had to keep certain records.

Undaunted, he borrowed money for a pushcart, prospered, bought other pushcarts, opened a store, enlarged it, and, in a small way, began dabbling in tenement real estate.

He was bright, quick, honest, and likable and within a dozen years was a major operator in tenement-house property. One day a terrific opportunity presented itself, one that required a tremendous amount of cash. Polansky applied at the East Side branch of a national bank, although he had never before borrowed extensively. However, his reputation preceded him and the bank was willing to make the loan.

"Glad to accommodate you," said the banker. "Here, just fill out this note for the amount."

Polansky smiled apologetically. "If you don't mind," he said, "you should, please, make out the note for me and I'll sign it."

"I don't understand," the banker said, puzzled.

"Well," sighed Polansky, "I have to tell you something. Myself, I can't read or write. Yetta, that's my wife, taught me how to make my own name on paper. But otherwise reading and writing by me is nix."

The banker stared, he was amazed.

"By heaven, that's a miracle! And yet, with such a handicap, in a few years you have made yourself a very rich man. It makes me wonder what you might have been in this country by now if you had been able to read and write."

"A *shammes*," said Polansky modestly.

■

A young Jewish philosophy student was invited by a pretty widow at a Washington political rally to guess her age.

"I have opposing ideas on that," he said, "I don't know whether to make you ten years younger on account of your looks, or ten years older on account of your brains."

■

The yeshiva student was new to the New York public school system and the questions on economics completely floored him. Statistics were not his meat. Yet he answered one very tough question correctly, if unexpectedly.

"State the number of tons of coal shipped out of the United States in a given year?"

He wrote: "1492—none."

■

The same student found a wallet with a ten-dollar bill in it and returned it to its owner—after first changing the bill into ten ones.

■

A very wealthy self-made man was asked the secret of his success. How had he made so much money? Were there any special rules?"

"Two," said the rich man. "What I had to do tomorrow, I did today. And what I had to eat today, I ate tomorrow."

■

GOOD
(Anonymous)

How are things?"

"Good."

"Good? With all the *tsouris* I know you have, how can they be good?"

"Always good—good—good. In the summer I'm good and hot. In the winter I'm good and cold. Because my roof leaks when it rains, I get good and wet. My *yenta* of a wife nags me until I'm good and mad. And in my miserable little hut I feel good and buried.

"Believe me, I'm good and sick of it all!"

Appendix A

Principal Writers of Jewish Humor of the Nineteenth Century

Since the eleventh century Jewish humor has been written in:

Hebrew	Arabic	Spanish
German	Danish	English
Russian	Hungarian	French
Yiddish	Dutch	

Except for a very few early writers (dates indicated) the majority of the following authors wrote nineteenth-century Jewish humor—the traditional humor of the European shtetl. Most of this is folk humor—anonymous funny stories, jokes, proverbs, witticisms, and epithets, which were passed along and embellished by generation after generation, frequently landing in this country with the immigrants.

AGNON, S.J. (CZACZKES), 1888–1970. Novelist. Born in Galicia, Austria; settled in Palestine. Wrote in Hebrew.

AL-CHARIZI, YEHUDAH, c. 1200. Poet. Born in Spain. Wrote in Hebrew.

ALTENBERG, PETER, 1859–1919. Humorist. Born in Vienna. Wrote in German.

ANSKY, S. (S.S. RAPOPORT), 1863–1920. Folklorist, poet, and dramatist. Wrote in Yiddish and Russian.

ASCH, SHOLEM, 1880–1957. Novelist, dramatist, and short-story writer. Born in Poland. Emigrated to the USA. Wrote in Yiddish.

BABEL, ISAAC, 1894–1941. Novelist and short-story writer. Wrote in Russian.

BAR-HEBRAEUS, 1226–1286. Physician and humorous anthologist. Son of converted Jew. Born in Syria. Rose to be head of the Eastern Jacobite church. Wrote in Arabic.

BENJACOB, ISAAC, 1801–1863. Poet and epigrammatist. Born in Lithuania. Wrote in Hebrew.

BERGELSON, DOVID, 1884–1952. Novelist, short-story writer, and dramatist. Born in Russia. Wrote in Yiddish.

BIALIK, HAYYIM NAHMAN, 1873–1934. Foremost Hebrew poet. Born in Russia, settled in Palestine. Wrote in Hebrew and in Yiddish.

BLOCH, JEAN-RICHARD, 1884–1947. Novelist, short-story writer, dramatist, and critic. Born in France. Wrote in French.

BÖRNE, LUDWIG (LÖB BARUCH), 1786–1837. Literary critic and political writer. Born in Germany. Wrote in German.

BRANDES, GEORG MORRIS (COHEN), 1842–1927. Literary critic, essayist, and biographer. Born in Denmark. Wrote in Danish.

DER LEBEDIGER (CHAIM GUTMAN), 1887–. Humorous writer. Born in Russia. Emigrated to USA. Wrote in Yiddish.

FEUCHTWANGER, LION, 1884–1958. Novelist, dramatist, and short-story writer. Born in Germany. Wrote in German.

FRANZOS, KARL EMIL, 1848–1904. Novelist, critic, and short-story writer. Born in Ukraine. Wrote in German.

FRUG, SIMEON SAMUEL, 1860–1916. Poet. Born in Russia. Wrote in Yiddish, Hebrew, and Russian.

GOLD, MICHAEL, 1894–1967. Novelist, playwright, and literary critic. Born in the USA. Wrote in English.

GOLDING, LOUIS, 1895–1958. Novelist, short-story writer, and poet. Born in England. Wrote in English.

GROPPER, JACOB, 1890–. Poet. Born in Bukovina, Austria. Wrote in Yiddish.

HA-LEVI, JUDAH, 1075–1141. Poet and philosopher. Born in Toledo, Spain. Wrote in Hebrew and Arabic.

HEIJERMANS, HERMAN, 1864–1924. Dramatist and novelist. Born in Holland. Wrote in Dutch.

HEINE, HEINRICH, 1797–1856. Lyric poet, prose satirist, and novelist. Born in Germany. Wrote in German.

IBN EZRA, ABRAHAM, 1090–1164. Poet and religious scholar. Born in Toledo, Spain. Wrote in Hebrew and Arabic.

KATZ, LEO, 1892–. Novelist, short-story writer, and journalist. Born in Bukovina, Austria. Settled in Vienna. Wrote in German and Yiddish.

KOBRIN, LEON, 1872–1946. Novelist, playwright, and short-story writer. Born in Russia. Emigrated to the USA. Wrote in Yiddish.

KOVNER, B. (JACOB ADLER), 1877–1974. Humorous writer. Born in Galicia, Austria. Emigrated to the USA. Wrote in Yiddish.

KRAUS, KARL, 1874–1936. Poet, dramatist, critic and journalist. Born in Prague, Austria. Wrote in German.

LEWISOHN, LUDWIG, 1882–1955. Novelist, critic, anthologist, translator, and teacher. Born in Berlin, Germany. Emigrated to the USA. Wrote in English.

LIBIN, Z. 1872–1955. Short-story writer and playwright. Born in Russia. Emigrated to the USA. Wrote in Yiddish.

MAIMON, SALOMON, 1753–1800. Philosopher. Born in Lithuania. Emigrated to Germany. Wrote in German.

MANDELKERN, SOLOMON, 1846–1902. Poet and Bible scholar. Born in Russia. Wrote in Hebrew, Yiddish, Russian, and German.

MENDELE MOKHER SEFARIM (SHALOM JACOB ABRAMOVICH), 1835–1917. Novelist, short-story writer, and satirist. Born in Russia. Wrote in Yiddish and Hebrew.

MOLNÁR, FERENC (NEUMANN), 1878–1952. Playwright. Born in Hungary. Wrote in Hungarian and German.

NADIR, MOISHE (ISAAC REISS), 1885–1943. Wit, satirist, poet, playwright, and critic. Born in Galicia, Austria. Emigrated to the USA. Wrote in Yiddish.

NORDAU, MAX SIMON (SÜDFELD), 1849–1923. Critic, historian, dramatist, philosopher, physician. Born in Hungary. Emigrated to Germany and France. Wrote in French and German.

OGUS, AARON D., 1865–1943. Humorous short-story writer. Born in Russia. Emigrated to the USA. Wrote in Yiddish.

PALQUERA, SHEMTOB, 1225–1290. Poet and philosopher. Born in Spain. Wrote in Hebrew.

PERETZ, I. L., 1852–1915. Short-story writer, poet, dramatist, critic, and essayist. Born in Poland. Wrote in Yiddish.

PREACHER OF DUBNO, THE (RABBI JACOB KRANTZ "DER DUBNER MAGOID") 1740–1804. Itinerant preacher. Born in Lithuania. Wrote in Hebrew.

REISEN, ABRAHAM, 1875–1935. Poet and short-story writer. Born in Russia. Emigrated to the USA. Wrote in Yiddish.

SAPHIR, MORITZ G., 1795–1858. Humorist. Born in Hungary, lived in Germany and Vienna. Wrote in German.

SCHENEOUR, ZALMAN, 1887–1959. Novelist, poet, and short-story writer. Born in Russia, lived in Germany, and then in the USA. Wrote in Hebrew and Yiddish.

SHOLEM ALEICHEM (SHOLEM RABINOWITZ), 1859–1916. Foremost humorist and satirist in modern Yiddish literature. Wrote novels, plays, short stories, monologues, sketches, etc. Born in Russia, died in New York. Wrote in Yiddish.

SPEKTOR, MORDCHE, 1858–1925. Novelist and short-story writer. Born in Russia. Emigrated to the USA. Wrote in Yiddish.

STEINBERG, ELIEZER, 1880–1932. Poet. Born in Russia. Emigrated to Brazil. Wrote in Yiddish.

STEINBERG, JACOB, 1886–1947. Poet. Born in Russia. Wrote in Hebrew and Russian.

STEINBERG, YEHUDAH, 1863–1908. Novelist and short-story writer. Born in Russia. Wrote in Hebrew and Yiddish.

SUHL, YURI, 1908–1986. Novelist in English and poet in Yiddish. Born in Galicia, Austria. Emigrated to the USA.

TASHRAK (ISRAEL JOSEPH ZEVIN), 1872–1926. Wrote humorous short stories and Talmudic anthologies. Born in Russia. Emigrated to the USA. Wrote in Yiddish.

TIEMPO, CESAR (ISRAEL ZEITLIN), 1906–. Poet and playwright. Born in Buenos Aires, Argentina. Wrote in Spanish.

UNTERMEYER, LOUIS, 1885–1977. Poet, critic, anthologist, and lecturer. Born in the USA. Wrote in English.

VULFARTS, M. Contemporary humorous writer. Born in Latvia. Writes in Yiddish.

WENDROFF, Z. (ZALMAN WENDROWSKY), 1879–1971. Humorous short-story writer. Born in Russia. Wrote in Yiddish.

WERFEL, FRANZ, 1890–1945. Poet, novelist, and dramatist. Born in Prague. Wrote in German.

WOLFE, HUMBERT, 1886–1940. Poet and translator. Born in England. Wrote in English.

YEHOASH (SOLOMON BLOOMGARDEN), 1870–1927. Poet, short-story writer, and Bible translator. Born in Russia. Emigrated to the USA. Wrote in Yiddish.

ZANGWILL, ISRAEL, 1864–1926. Novelist, short-story writer, playwright, and essayist. Noted Jewish leader. Born in London. Wrote in English.

Appendix B

An American Jewish Humor Honor Roll

Selecting material for a book of Jewish humor is, fortunately, a selection from among riches rather than a scrabble with poverty. But because there is so much to choose from, we must perforce narrow our sights and leave out large and important categories—like essays, short stories, and excerpts from novels.

In addition to space being limited, this is, after all, primarily a "joke book" rather than an anthology of lengthier pieces. So while we are singing the praises of several celebrated Jewish writers, and urging that you read them, we are not including samples of their work.

The prominence of Jewish writers in American literature since 1900 is nothing short of amazing when we consider that barely two percent of our population is Jewish! Inevitably, great writers leap to mind, humorists and others:

S. J. Perelman, Arthur Kober, Samuel Hoffenstein, Leo Rosten, Dorothy Parker, Edna Ferber, Irwin Shaw, Fannie Hurst, Herman Wouk, Jerome Weidman, Saul Bellow, Herbert Gold, Isaac Bashevis Singer, Philip Roth, and Joseph Heller....

Any research in depth would undoubtedly double the list. Our serious recommendation: Read them all!

Comic Strips

Jewish humor was prevalent here: "Krazy Kat" by George Herriman; Al Capp's "Li'l Abner'; Bud Fisher's "Mutt & Jeff";

Rube Goldberg's maniacal inventions; Harry Hirschfield's "Abie the Agent."...

In addition to syndicated newspaper strips, there were single frames, with or without "balloons" for a character's thoughts or speech. For generations these convulsed readers of the *Saturday Evening Post, Look, Liberty, Esquire,* and *The New Yorker.* These leading cartoonists were (and are) all Jewish: Hoff, Steig, Soglow, Steinberg, Hirschfeld, in addition to many others less famous.

Records and Popular Sheet Music
These were practically a Jewish monopoly, sung and played everywhere, written by the legendary Irving Berlin, Ira Gershwin, Lorenz Hart, Harry Ruby, Dorothy Fields, Howard Dietz, E.Y. "Yip" Harburg....

Vaudeville
This was possibly the most influential of the popular arts during the early twentieth century, containing an astonishing number of Jewish performers. Their names (and acts) are still legends: Smith and Dale, Potash and Perlmutter, George Jessel, The Ritz Brothers, The Four Marx Brothers, Milton Berle, Jack Benny, George Burns, Willie and Eugene Howard, Eddie Cantor, Lou Holtz....

And as you can imagine, their skits, gags, dialogues, and routines were written largely by Jewish gag writers.

Broadway and Musical Comedies
From vaudeville the leading performers became stars in comedies and "musicals" that toured the country with road companies. Jewish wit and humor poured from the typewriters of Ben Hecht, George S. Kaufman, Moss Hart, Alan Jay Lerner, Morrie Ryskind, Oscar Hammerstein II, Abe Burrows, and Neil Simon to name a few....

Radio
This medium, brought to commercial success by Jews David Sarnoff and William Paley, rapidly took on the popular per-

formers of vaudeville, the stage, and the movies, including Fanny Brice, Jack Benny, Ed Wynn, and George Burns....

Networked across America, now the tiniest hamlet looked forward to Gertrude Berg ("Mollie Goldberg") and Milton Berle. The radio comedy writers, later to graduate to TV's sitcoms, and often to assume acting roles themselves, included such writers as Woody Allen, Mel Brooks, Carl Reiner, Nat Perrin, and Milt Josefsberg.

Moving Pictures

Movies were started on the East Coast, and the great majority of the pioneer moving-picture producers were Jewish businessmen—clothing manufacturers and theater owners: Mayer, Lasky, Goldwyn, Fox, Warner, Zukor, Laemmle. But they grew and developed in California because of its superior climate and filming conditions. Jewish writers poured into Hollywood and included all the known writers plus newcomers who had never written for vaudeville, Broadway, radio, or anything else.

Television

Most of the shows that *launched* TV as a mass medium were written by Jews: "The Texaco Star Theater," "The Colgate Comedy Hour," starring Fred Allen, "The Jack Benny Show," "The Milton Berle Show," "Your Show of Shows."

The preponderance of television sitcoms were written by battalions of Jewish gag writers, credited various ways, including "story by," "written by," "story consultant," or "story supervision." Under such attributions, comedy "greats" like Larry Gelbart and Norman Lear worked their magic.

The names of the multimillion-audience shows are legend today: "The Carol Burnett Show," "The Mary Tyler Moore Show," "All in the Family," "M*A*S*H," "The Odd Couple," "I Love Lucy," "The Honeymooners," "Barney Miller," "Sergeant Bilko," "The Phil Silvers Show," "Roseanne."

It is little wonder that so many of the plots and characters bear the clear imprint of Jewish humor.

The Joke's on Us
More Humor Books From Carol Publishing Group!

Ask for the books listed below at your bookstore. Or to order direct from the publisher call 1-800-447-BOOK (MasterCard or Visa) or send a check or money order for the books purchased (plus $3.00 shipping and handling for the first book ordered and 50¢ for each additional book) to Carol Publishing Group, 120 Enterprise Avenue, Dept. 1503, Secaucus, NJ 07094.

Advanced Backstabbing and Mudslinging Techniques by George Hayduke, paperback $7.95 (#40560)

The Best Book of Puns by Art Moger, paperback $7.95 (#51097)

The Complete Pun Book by Art Moger, paperback $8.95 (#50776)

501 Survival Tips for Men: Making Your Way in a World Full of Women by Craig Hartglass, paperback $8.95 (#51504)

Getting Even by George Hayduke, oversized paperback $12.95 (#40314)

Getting Even 2 by George Hayduke, oversized paperback $12.95 (#40337)

The Giant Book of Insults by Louis A. Safian, paperback $7.95 (#50881)

Great Lawyer Stories, compiled by Bill Adler, paperback $7.95 (#51373)

Henny Youngman's Giant Book of Jokes, paperback $6.95 (#50854)

How to be a Stand-up Comic by Richard Belzer, paperback $9.95 (#51319)

How to Make Your Analyst Love You by Theodor Saretsky, paperback $7.95 (#51412)

It's Impossible to Learn Elevator Repair From Your Mother, by R.S. Bean, paperback $9.95 (#51327)

The Limerick paperback $12.95 (#50713)

Prices subject to change;
books subject to availability

Make 'em Pay by George Hayduke, paperback $7.95 (#40421)

Make My Day by George Hayduke, paperback $7.95 (#40464)

Mayhem by George Hayduke, paperback $7.95 (#40565)

More of the World's Best Dirty Jokes by Mr. "J", paperback $5.95 (#50710)

The North Dakota Joke Book by Mike Dalton, paperback $7.95 (#51041)

Revenge by George Hayduke, oversized paperback $14.95 (#40353)

Righteous Revenge by George Hayduke, paperback $8.95 (#40569)

Some Day My Prince Will Come: A Guide for Women Whose Dream Has Not Yet Come True by Serena Gray, paperback $10.95 (#51510)

Still More of the World's Best Dirty Jokes by Mr. "J", paperback $3.95 (#50834)

The World's Best Irish Jokes by Mr. "O's", paperback $4.95 (#50861)

The World's Best Jewish Humor by Stanley A. Kramer, paperback $8.95 (#51503)

The World's Best Russian Underground Jokes by Algis Ruksenas , paperback $5.95 (#50994)

The World's Dirtiest Dirty Jokes by Mr. "J", paperback $7.95 (#51478)

The World's Greatest Golf Jokes by Stan McDougal, paperback $4.95 (#50831)